THE ESSENTIAL

STOWE HOUSE

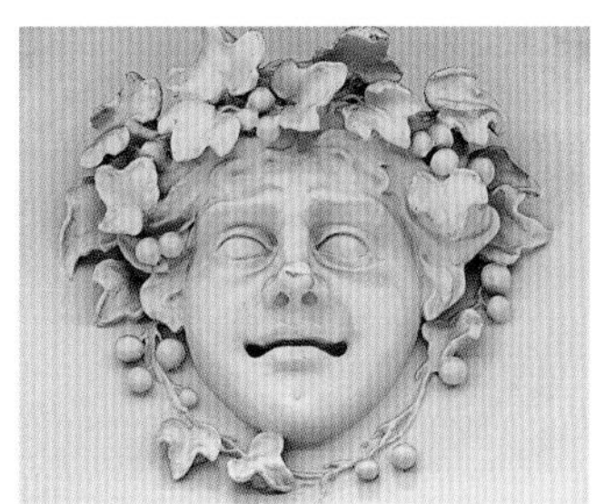

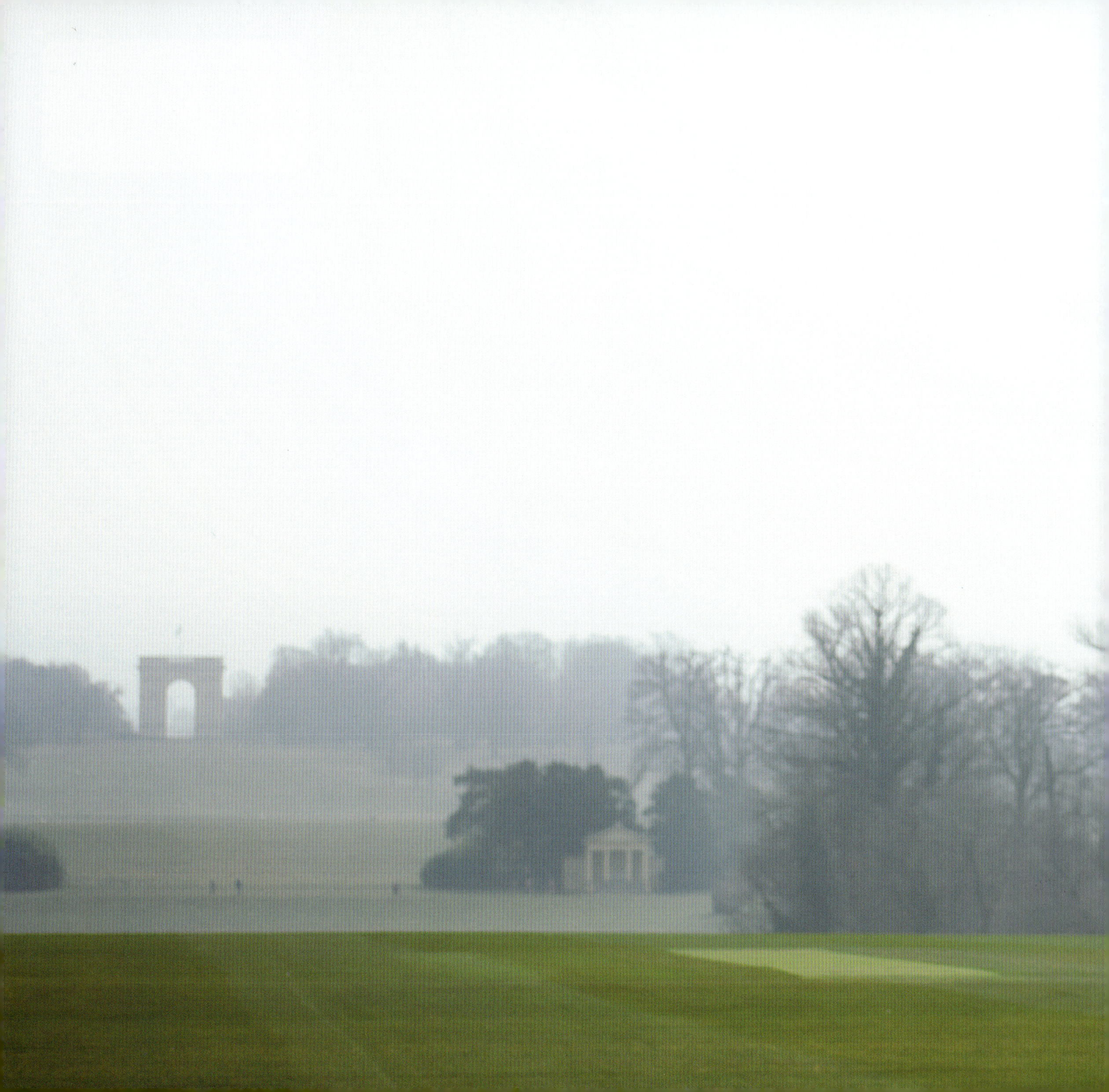

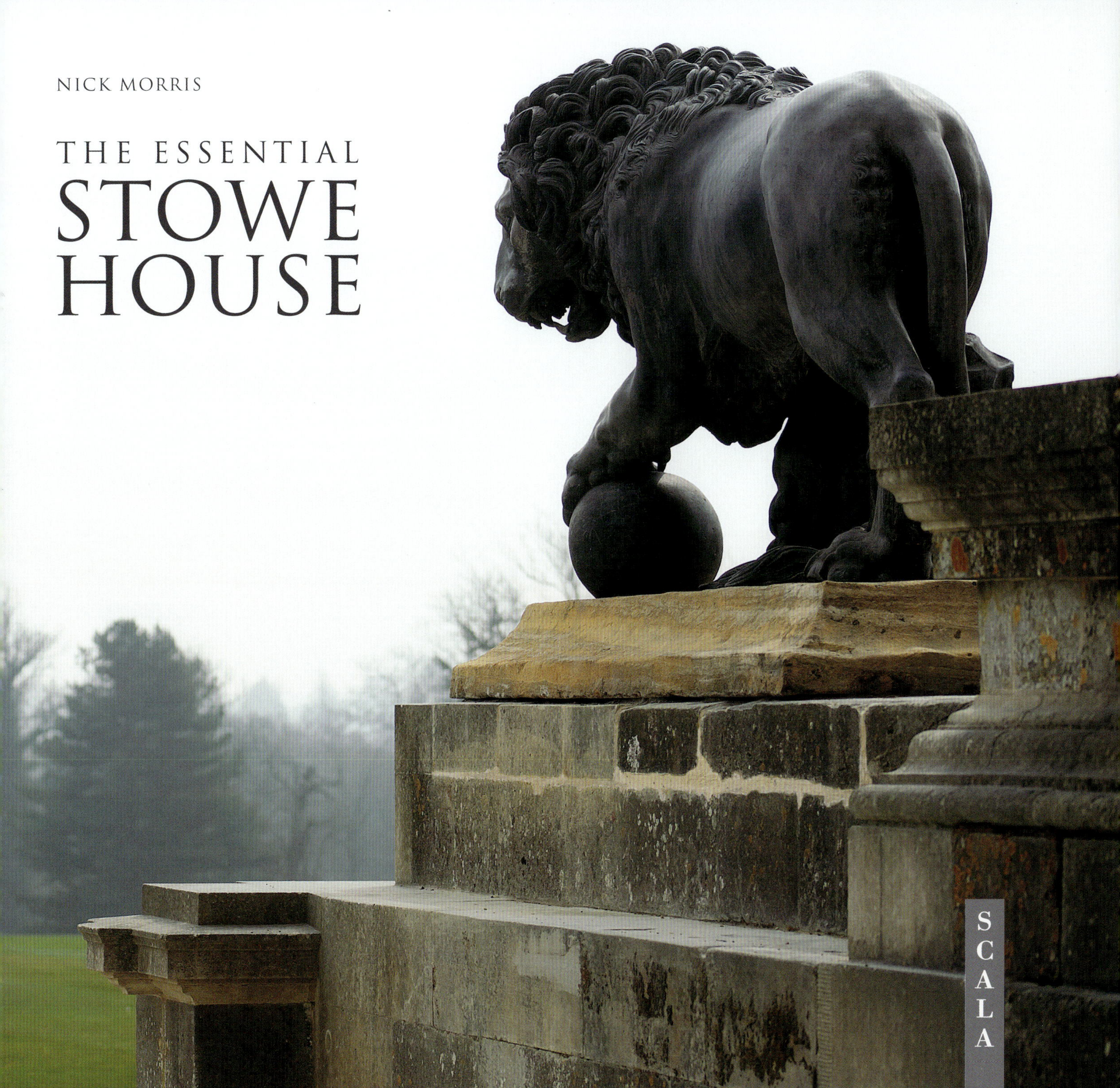
NICK MORRIS
THE ESSENTIAL
STOWE
HOUSE
SCALA

This edition © Scala Arts & Heritage Publishers Ltd, 2015
Text © Stowe House Preservation Trust, 2015

First published in 2015 by
Scala Arts & Heritage Publishers Ltd
10 Lion Yard
Tremadoc Road
London SW4 7NQ, UK
www.scalapublishers.com

In association with
Stowe School
Stowe
Buckingham MK18 5EH, UK
www.stowe.co.uk

ISBN 978-1-85759-938-1

Project manager and copy editor: Linda Schofield
Designed by Maggi Smith
Printed in Turkey

10 9 8 7 6 5 4 3 2 1

Front cover: The North Front
Back cover: The Marble Saloon
Frontispiece: The lions overlooking the Landscape Gardens
Contents page: The ceiling of the State Drawing Room (now known as the Temple Room)

Picture Credits
All © Andy Marshall, apart from the following:

Front cover and pages 10 (bottom), 13, 29 (left), 35 (top centre and right): © Stowe School Ltd
Page 8: © Bruce White
Page 10 (top): © Historic England
Pages 11, 24 (Temple of Concord and Victory, and Gothic Temple), 26, 27, 36 (bottom left and right), 43 (left): © Nick Morris
Page 29 (right): Royal Collection Trust / © Her Majesty Queen Elizabeth II 2015
Page 31 (right): © R. & H. Chapman (Buckingham)
Page 35 (top left): © Portmeirion Ltd
Page 36 (top): © Stowe School Ltd (photo: Ben Andrews)
Pages 38 (left and right), 39 (top): © Stowe School Ltd (photo: Alan Longworth)
Pages 44, 45 (top left): © Kiffy Stainer Hutchins Ltd
Inside back cover (plan of Stowe House): © Stowe House Preservation Trust

CONTENTS

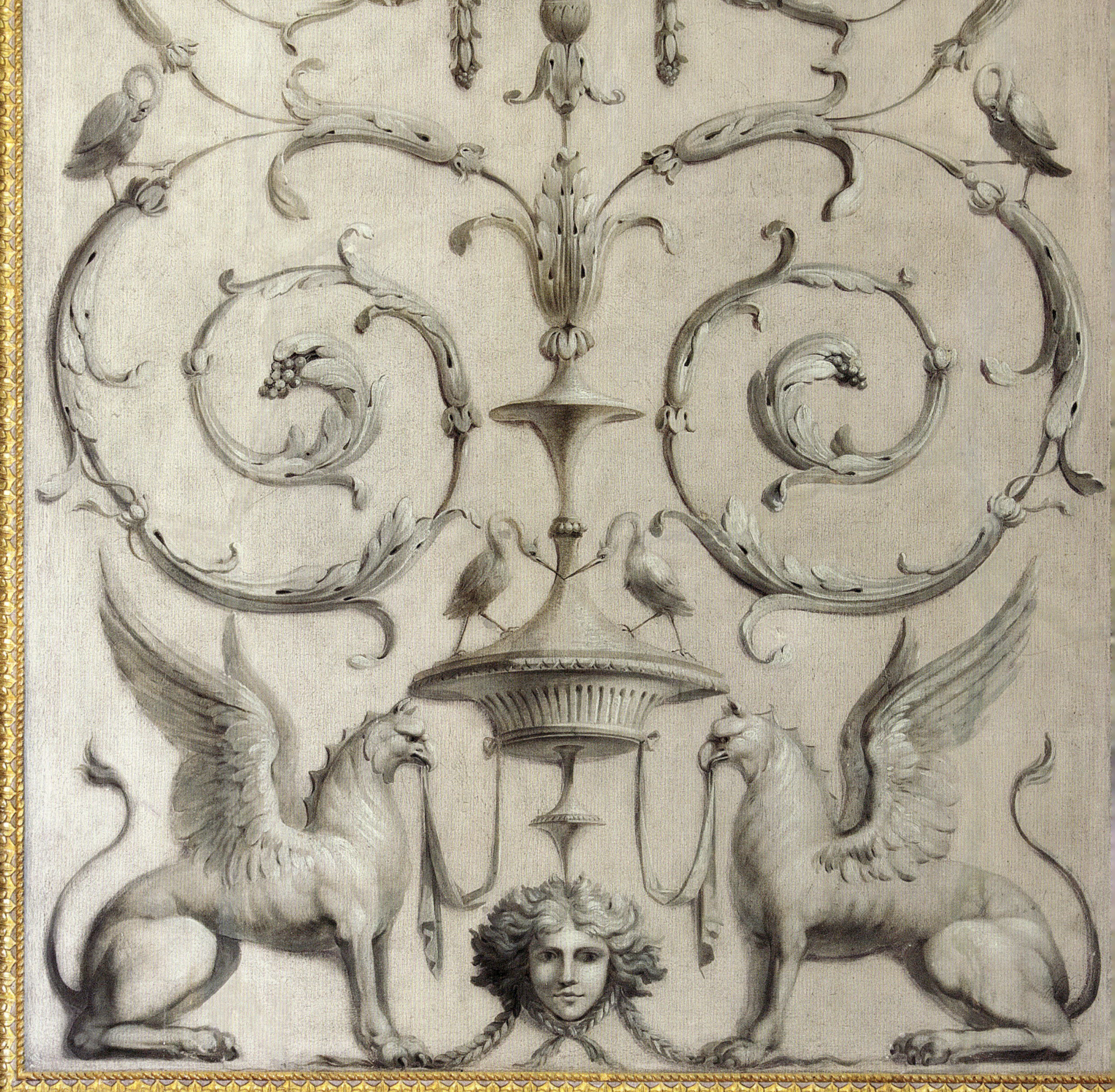

FOREWORD AND ACKNOWLEDGEMENTS

Stowe is the largest private Neo-Classical building in Europe: a place of inspiration, where ideas, power and architecture combined to create the majestic seat of one of Britain's most prominent eighteenth-century families. Producing four Prime Ministers and many government ministers, the Temple-Grenville family built Stowe to entertain and impress, informed by concepts, ideas and design from around the world and throughout history. The House is the grandest temple in the Landscape Gardens, where 30 other buildings, influenced by cultures from the ancient world to China, served practical, ornamental and symbolic purposes. At the heart of everything lie notions of political liberty, choice and good governance but, above all, creativity reigns and shows the real capacity of such talent to move, enthuse and exhilarate us. Today, Stowe School maintains the traditions of respect for the individual, the excitement of learning and the value of achievement. A spirit of enlightenment still pervades the site and we hope that time spent here will inspire visitors to realise their own creative potential.

I would like to thank the following for their work on this book: Andy Marshall, for his wonderful photography; Linda Schofield, for her patience and support as editor; and Michael Bevington, Martin Drury, Sandra Ellerby, Andrew Fane, Christopher Honeyman Brown, Anna McEvoy, Janice Morris, Rosie Morris, Crispin Robinson, Tori Roddy, Jenna Spellane and Anthony Wallersteiner, for their various and much appreciated contributions.

Nick Morris
CEO Stowe House Preservation Trust
January 2015

Detail of griffins in the State Music Room.

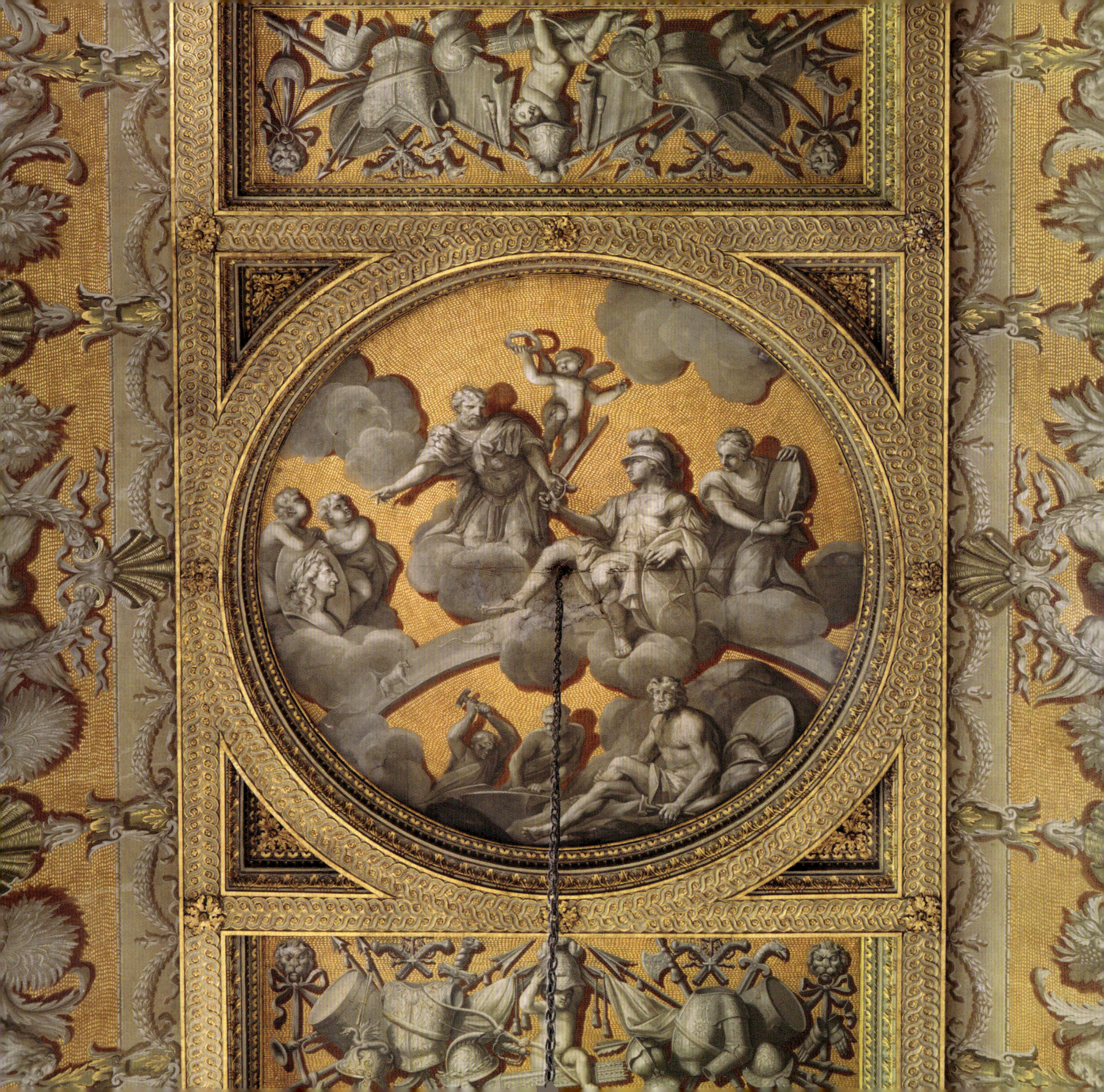

1 CREATION

The Creation of an Estate and Political Dynasty
In 1571 Peter Temple took a lease on land for sheep farming at Stowe in Buckinghamshire. Within 250 years, his family had risen through the ranks of the nobility, becoming the Dukes of Buckingham and Chandos and enlarging the family name to Temple-Nugent-Brydges-Chandos-Grenville. In the process, they created Stowe's world-famous Landscape Gardens with Stowe House, a palatial mansion, at the core.

The family claimed descent from the Saxon Earls of Mercia and their ambition is clear to see from the way they sought power and visibility on the local stage as a prelude to national prominence. In this, Peter and his descendants were helped by the proximity of the 'rotten borough' of Buckingham, with its 13 voters, which offered an easy way into politics and, with it, fame and influence.

The lease was inherited by Peter Temple's son, John, described as 'frugal and provident',[1] and, after him, by his son Thomas, a very different character who was appointed a Justice of the Peace and High Sheriff of Buckinghamshire.

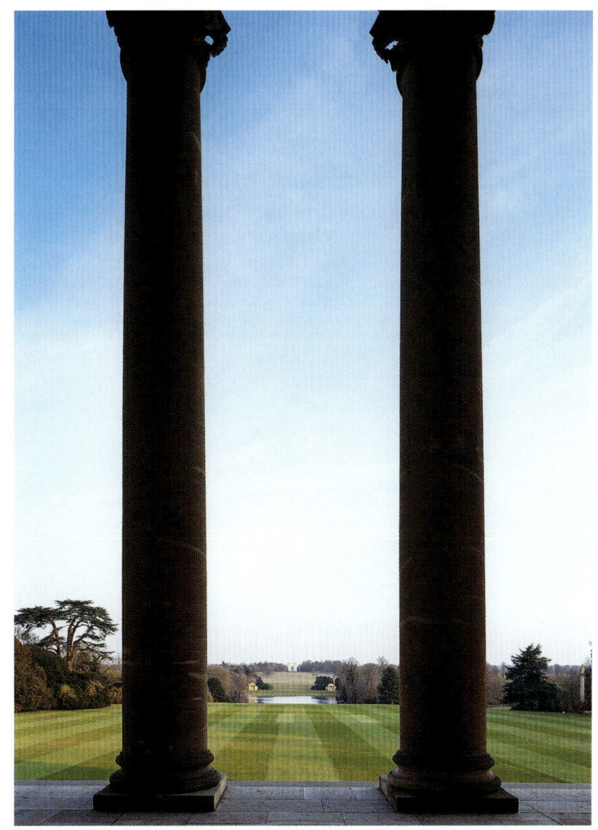

OPPOSITE
The North Hall ceiling with Viscount Cobham seated and receiving a sword from King William III dressed as Mars, god of war.

RIGHT
A view from the House to the Corinthian Arch in the distance.

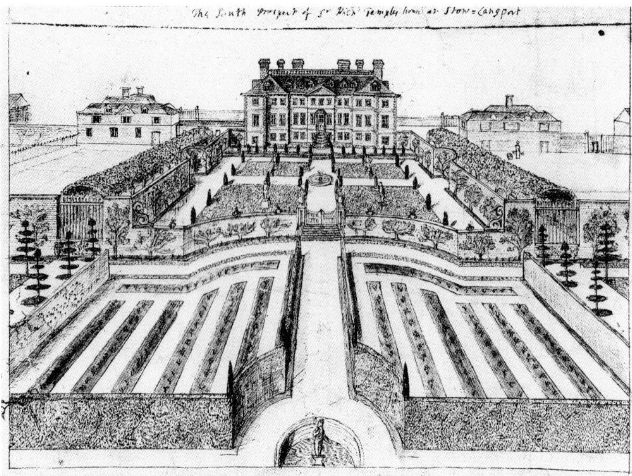

LEFT
View of the house designed by William Cleare for Sir Richard Temple, 1686.

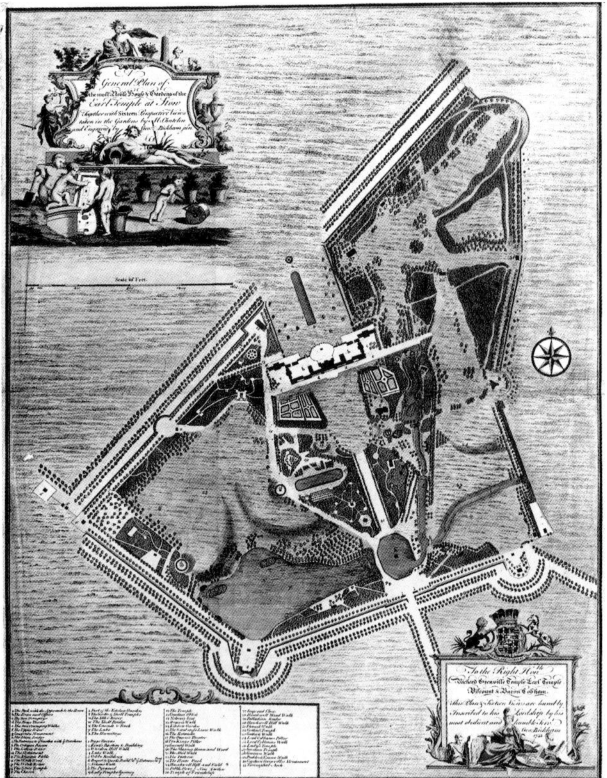

BELOW LEFT
Plan of the Stowe Estate first drawn by Sarah Bridgeman in 1739 and updated by George Bickham in 1753.

In an overt show of ambition, Thomas bought a knighthood in 1603 and a baronetcy in 1611, becoming 1st Baronet. His eldest son, Peter, acquired the Estate in 1630 and became the 2nd Baronet, having sued his father Sir Thomas who, in selling land at Stowe to add to another of his estates, had contravened an agreement into which father and son had previously entered. Through marriage to Anne Throckmorton, Sir Thomas had already gained the Luffield Estate to the north of Stowe, thus beginning a process of enlarging the Estate that would continue for over 200 years.

It was Sir Richard Temple, 3rd Baronet, who, between 1677 and 1683, laid the foundations for the House that we see today. Tearing down the former medieval manor (the site of which has never been found, but is believed to lie close to Stowe Parish Church to the south-east of the present property), he built a house to designs by William Cleare, the master joiner who had made the model for Sir Christopher Wren's St Paul's Cathedral. The contract, dated 1676, records the names of John Heynes (carpenter) and Thomas Miller (bricklayer) as parties to the agreement with Sir Richard Temple to construct 'a greate Messuage Mantion House of Brick (and other materials) ornamented with free stone'. At a cost of £26,000, Sir Richard's first residence was impressive, although it would be eclipsed by today's House. A drawing from about 1686 shows this substantial building from the South Front, with a pump on the right-hand side

RIGHT
Under the basement floor, a well was discovered in the summer of 2011, reflecting the position of a pump in the 1686 drawing opposite.

BELOW RIGHT
From high above the Landscape Gardens, Viscount Cobham surveys his creation.

reflecting the position of a well discovered under the present House in 2011.

Expansion – Viscount Cobham

Sir Richard's son, also Sir Richard (made Viscount Cobham in 1718) took the initial steps to creating today's House, a task that would bring a succession of famous architects to Stowe over the next 100 years. First on the scene was Sir John Vanbrugh, a fellow member of the Kit-Cat Club. This was a cultured group founded by London-based bookseller Jacob Tonson in the late 1690s, initially as a means of developing promising young writers; it subsequently became a forum for the discussion of politics, literature, architecture and current affairs over a bottle or two of wine and a mutton pie. Its members included the poet William Congreve, who is commemorated in one of Stowe's garden monuments, along with Joseph Addison and Richard Steele, authors of *The Tatler*.[2] Viscount Cobham's nephew, who would subsequently inherit Stowe, was also a member and, along with fellow political supporters of Cobham, became one of a group known as 'Cobham's Cubs'. Stowe's North Portico is attributed to Vanbrugh, who said in 1711 of porticos that 'no production in architecture is so solemnly magnificent'.[3] It is likely that Vanbrugh was also behind plans drawn up in 1719–20 to meet Viscount Cobham's vision for his house and grounds. A bird's-eye view in the Bodleian

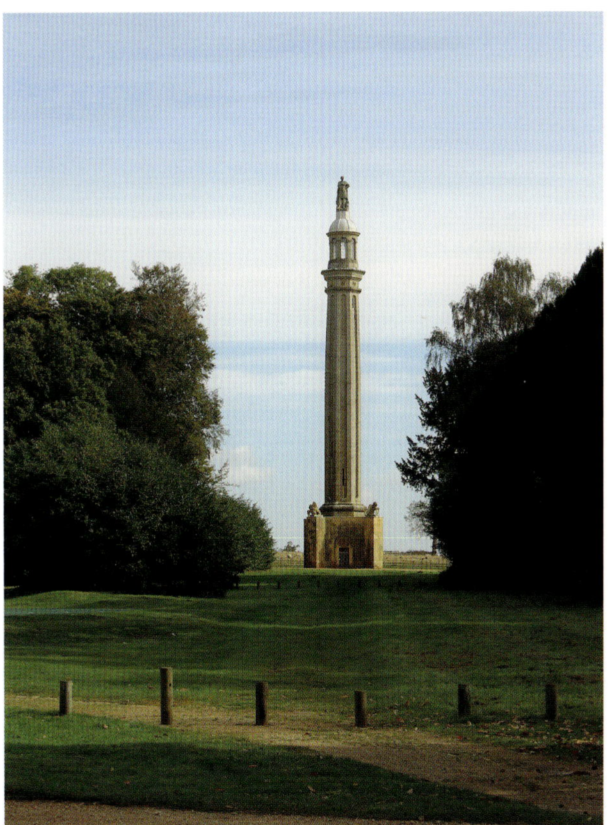

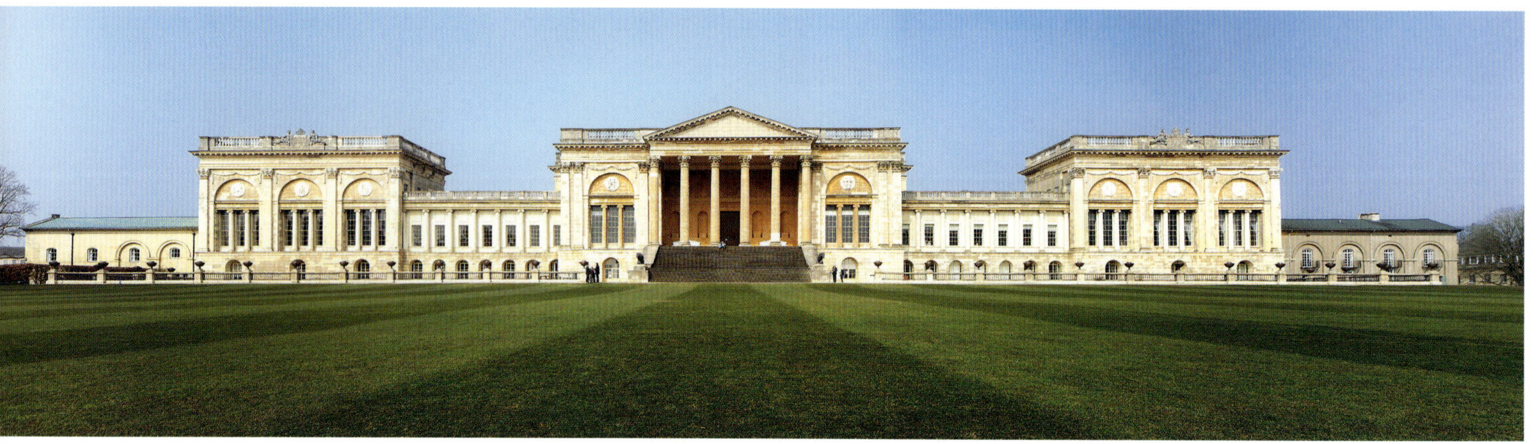

Stowe House's majestic South Front, which was rebuilt between 1771 and 1779 to a design by Thomas Pitt, Earl Temple's cousin.

OPPOSITE
The colonnades sweeping towards the North Portico, which is as solemn and magnificent as Vanbrugh intended.

Library shows a house with many features associated with Vanbrugh's architectural style, notably turrets on the four corners and two flanking pavilions that survive to this day in the service wings at the extremities of the main House. Viscount Cobham was a successful soldier and politician, serving under the Duke of Marlborough and reaching the rank of Lieutenant-General in 1710 at the age of 34. Stowe's Landscape Gardens are largely his creation and full of allusions to his political beliefs. Three paths, described in the National Trust guide, outline the ways of Vice, Virtue and Liberty, all reflected in the buildings and landscape along the way. Vice suggests lust and illicit or unhappy love, Virtue alludes to Greek and Saxon values and Liberty charts the origins of English political liberty.

The Architectural Cast

Vanbrugh was succeeded by a number of celebrated architects and designers of the age, among them William Kent, James Gibbs, Giacomo Leoni, Robert Adam, Giovanni Battista Borra, Vincenzo Valdrè and Sir John Soane, all of whom had a hand in remodelling parts of the House and grounds. By the middle of the eighteenth century, however, as a result of successive additions and changes, the South Front appeared disorderly and haphazard. These were far from the qualities that accorded with Georgian ideas on architecture, prizing as they did order and harmony, but it would fall to Cobham's successor to effect the changes needed to bring the House up to the style of the day.

Succession

Viscount Cobham died childless in 1749 and the House and gardens passed to his nephew, Richard Grenville, created Earl Temple soon afterwards. An active politician, he became a Knight of the Garter in 1760, an award proudly commemorated in the inclusion of the Order's insignia on the ceiling of the State Bedchamber. Such was his dislike of Earl Temple, it is said that King George II, rather than bestowing the honour in the usual fashion, tossed the ribbon to the recipient in a disdainful manner. Earl Temple used his considerable wealth to expand Stowe, rebuilding the North and South Fronts. To the north, he added the curved colonnades that embrace the carriage drive leading

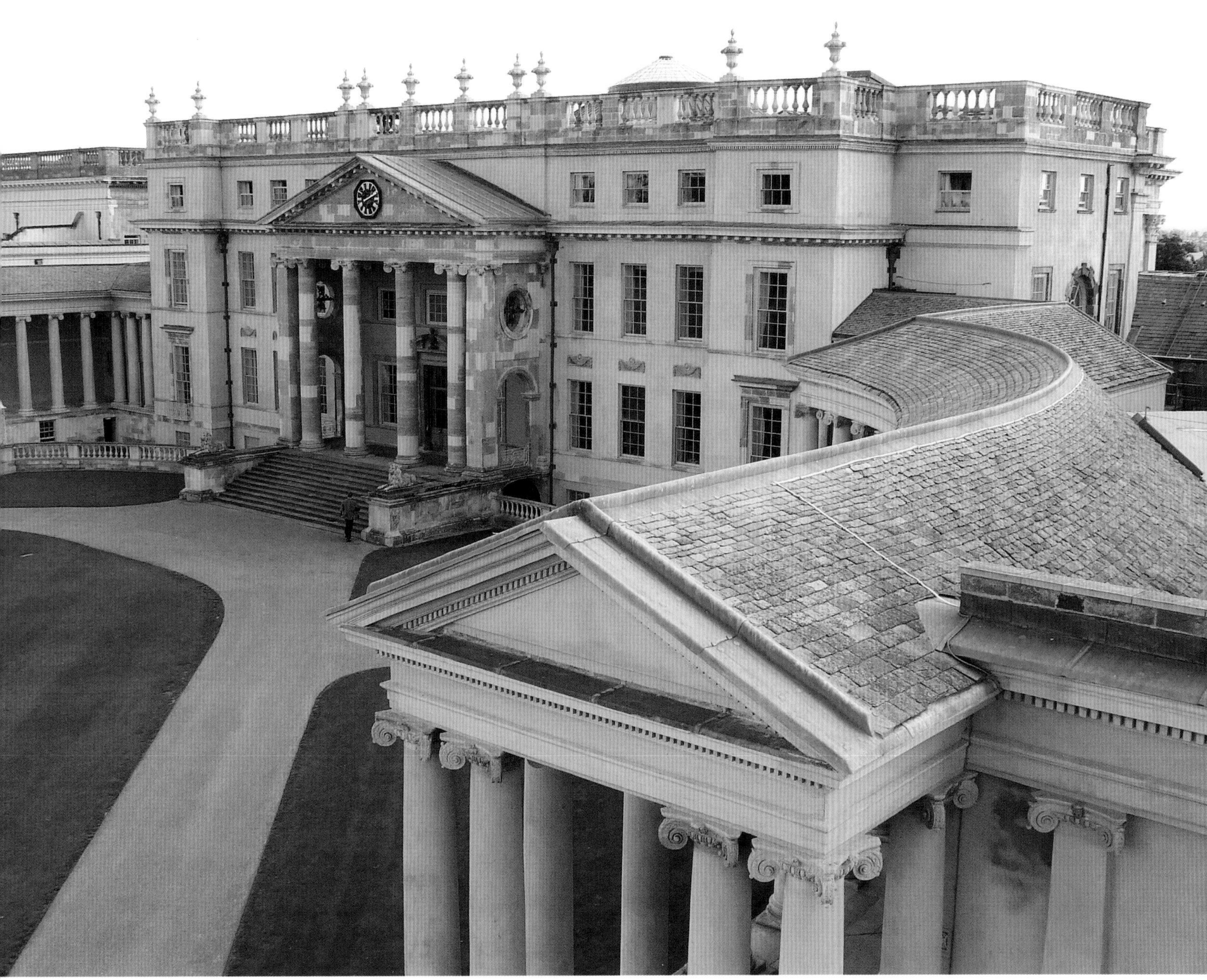

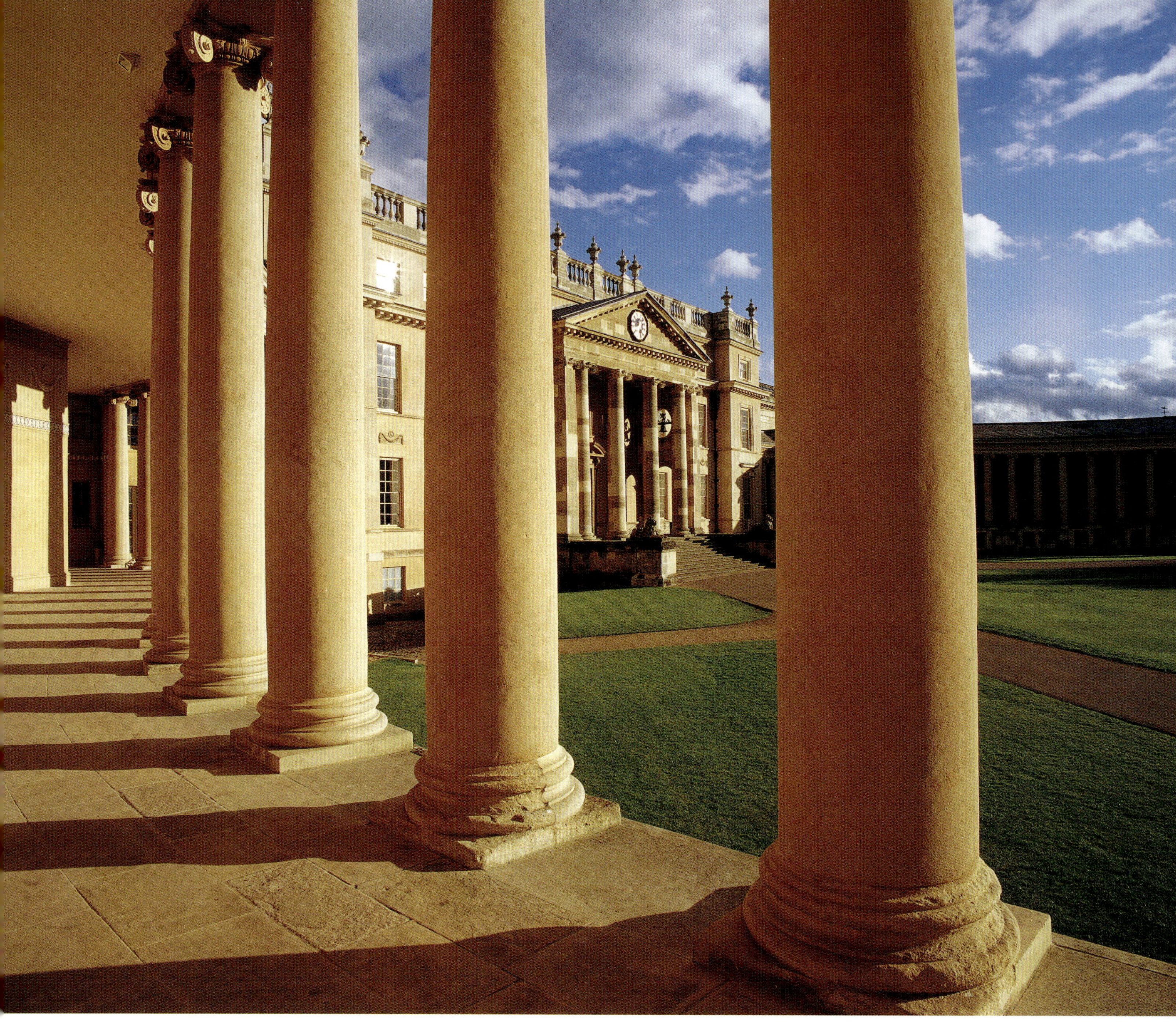

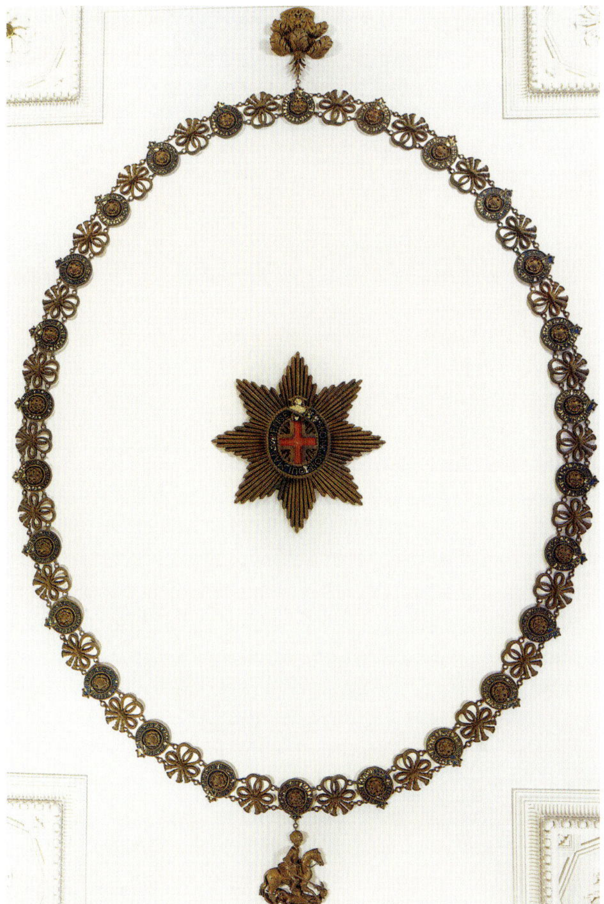

OPPOSITE
The elegant, curving colonnades were added to the North Front during Earl Temple's time.

LEFT
The insignia of the Order of the Garter, proudly displayed on the ceiling of the former State Bedchamber.

BELOW
A Bacchic scene featured in the South Portico, possibly representing Earl Temple feeding the lion.

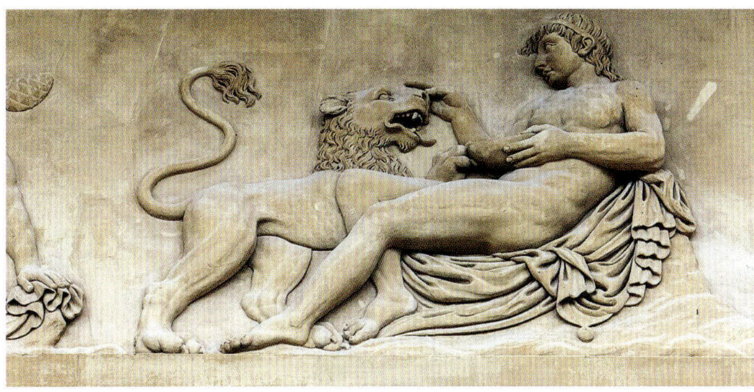

to the House and, although technically Cobham was not entitled to call his House a Palace (that was reserved for kings and princes of the Church), the term began to be used to describe his residence. At 192 metres in length, the grand enfilade of State Rooms and the associated service wings were impressive but in need of stylistic unity. Several architects were engaged to redesign the South Front. In 1771 Robert Adam submitted a proposal that was judged too fussy. It was improved by Thomas Pitt, Lord Camelford (Earl Temple's cousin), to the one that today stands above the surrounding gardens, providing the harmony and coherence that would bring Stowe up to the latest standards in taste. Under the South Front Portico a Bacchic feast is featured, another allusion to the classical world, though it has also been suggested that the long-limbed gentleman feeding the lion might represent Earl Temple, whose legs led to the nicknames 'Long Legs Temple' and 'Squire Gawky'.

Earl Temple's work was completed by his nephew, George Grenville, who took the family standing one rank higher when he was created Marquess of Buckingham in 1784. He did not enjoy the political success of his uncle but served two stints as Lord Lieutenant of Ireland and was greatly enriched through possession of Tellerships of the Exchequer, that is, sinecures obtained through family influence that returned a payout from government contracts. In peacetime this resulted in an income of about £3,000 per annum, but during the Napoleonic and American Wars it increased beyond measure. By 1808 his share of income

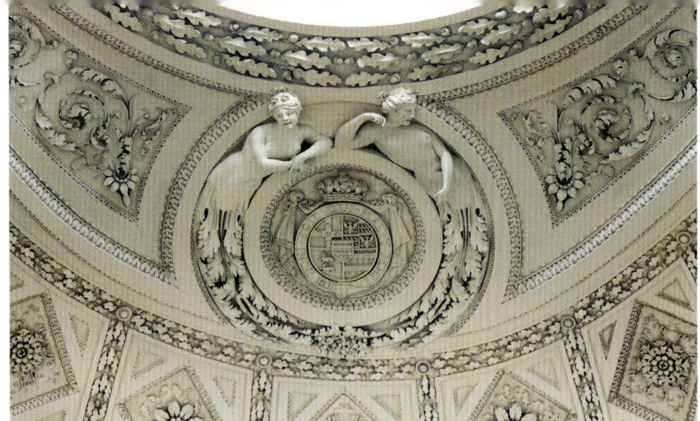

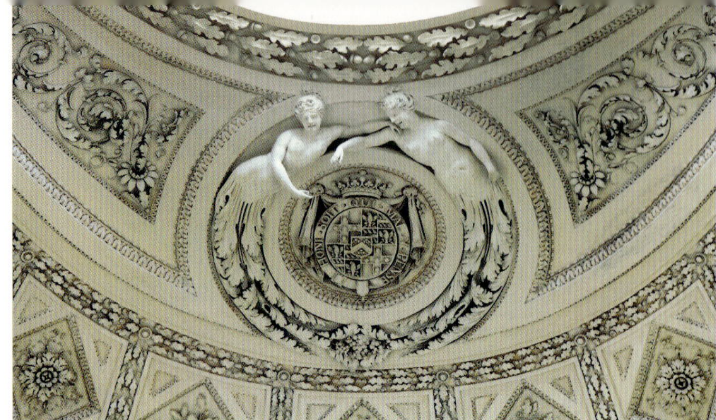

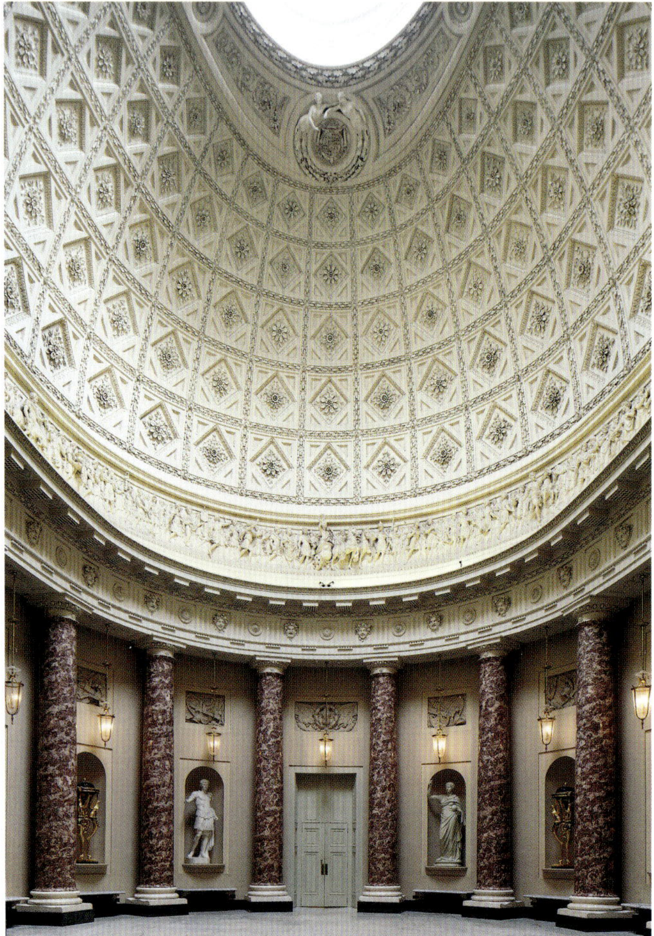

from this source was reported by the Committee on Public Expenditure to be £23,000, and between 1793 and 1812 it averaged £14,471 (about £1.5m today).

Remodelling the Interiors

The interiors of the House were also remodelled by the Marquess, most notably the Marble Saloon, which, in 1774, replaced the Great Parlour, with a design based on the Pantheon in Rome, rising to a 17-metre dome and costing £12,000. High in the ceiling, the coats of arms of Earl Temple and the Marquess of Buckingham symbolise their roles in planning and executing the designs, while the niches around the walls housed statues acquired on his Grand Tour by the Marquess to orders placed by his uncle. The design of the Saloon is attributed to Georges-Francois Blondel but the details are believed to have come from Vincenzo Valdrè, a little-known but endearing Italian artist. He worked extensively for the Marquess both at Stowe and in Ireland. In the grounds, Valdrè built two lodges and the Ménagerie and re-modelled the base of Lord Cobham's monument, but he is best remembered for the State Music Room. Its walls recall classical scenes in a playful take on Pompeian

ABOVE
The arms of Earl Temple (left) and the Marquess of Buckingham (right) commemorate the roles of both in planning and executing the work.

LEFT
The Marble Saloon, with its coffered ceiling, was modelled on the Pantheon in Rome and houses classical statues in the niches around its circumference.

The eight classical statues in the niches around the Marble Saloon are copies of the kind of statues that George Grenville would have procured for his uncle Earl Temple. They were installed in 2009 and their acquisition was made possible by the generosity of the Hall Bequest Trust.

TOP, LEFT TO RIGHT
A typical Roman senator in his toga and holding a scroll.

Hygeia, the Greek goddess of health.

Antinous, a young man of numerous talents whose friendship with the Emperor Hadrian led to his deification after his death in the river Nile.

Venus, Roman goddess of love, also associated with beauty and fertility.

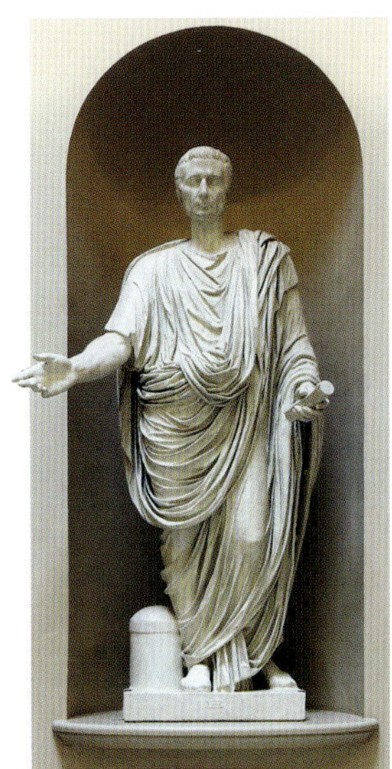
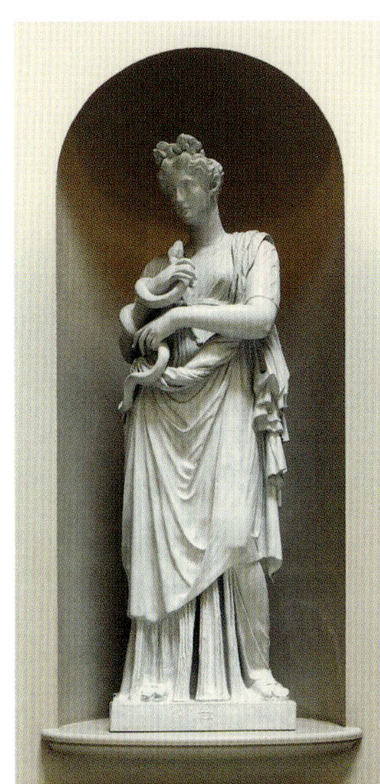
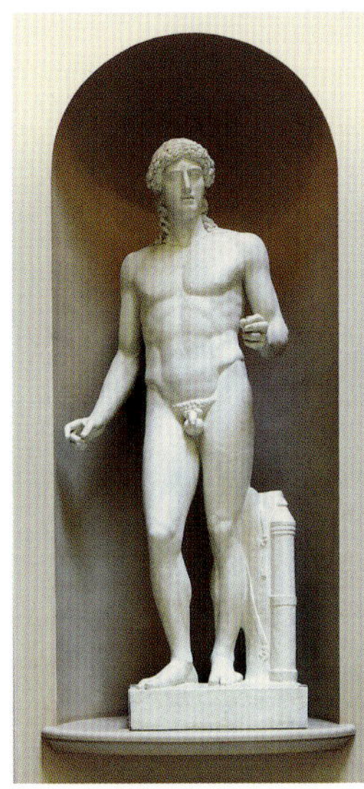
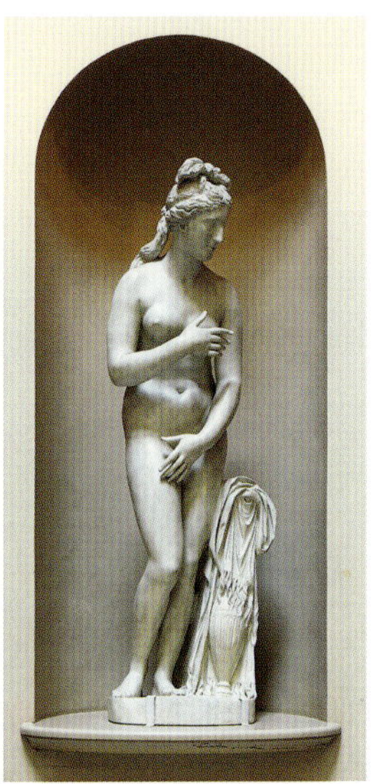

LEFT TO RIGHT
Augustus, the first Emperor of Rome after the fall of the Republic.

Apollo, the son of Zeus and Leto, was the god of music and often depicted with a lyre.

Urania, the muse of astronomy and astrology, holding a globe.

Meleager, a hunter prince whose death was foretold at his birth.

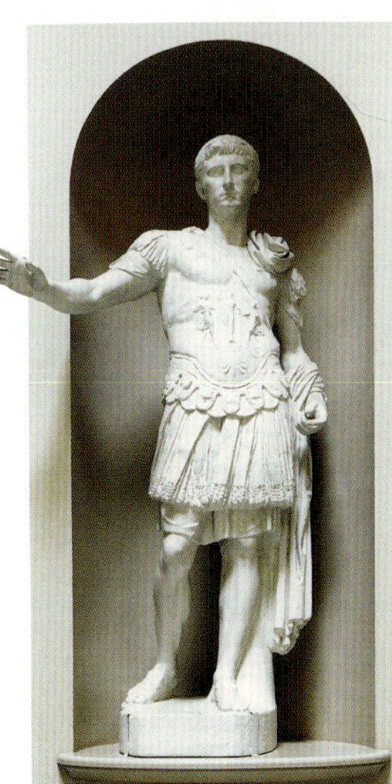
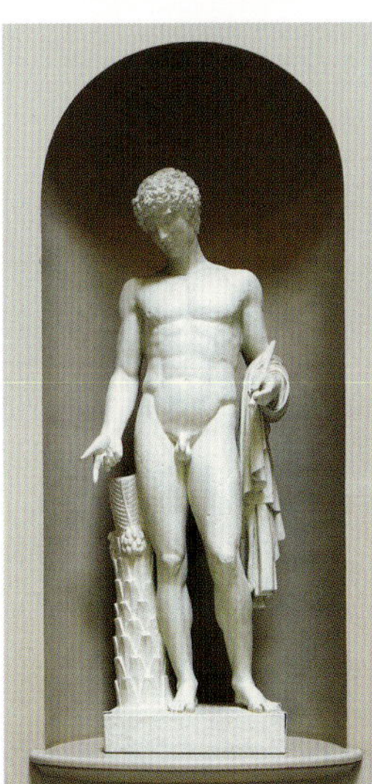
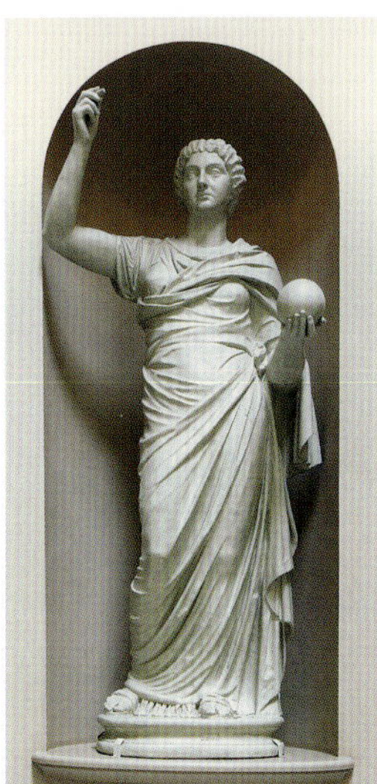
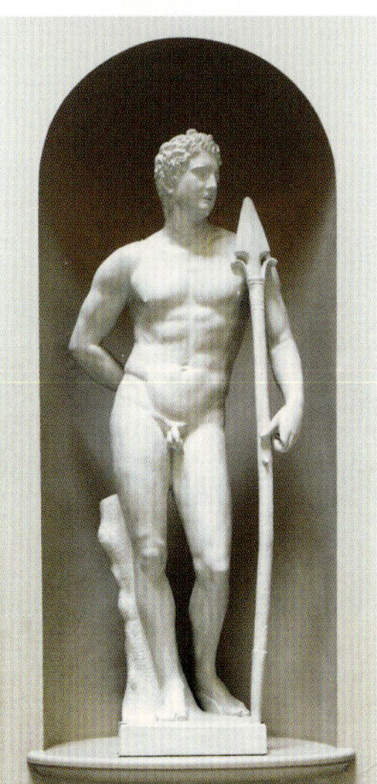

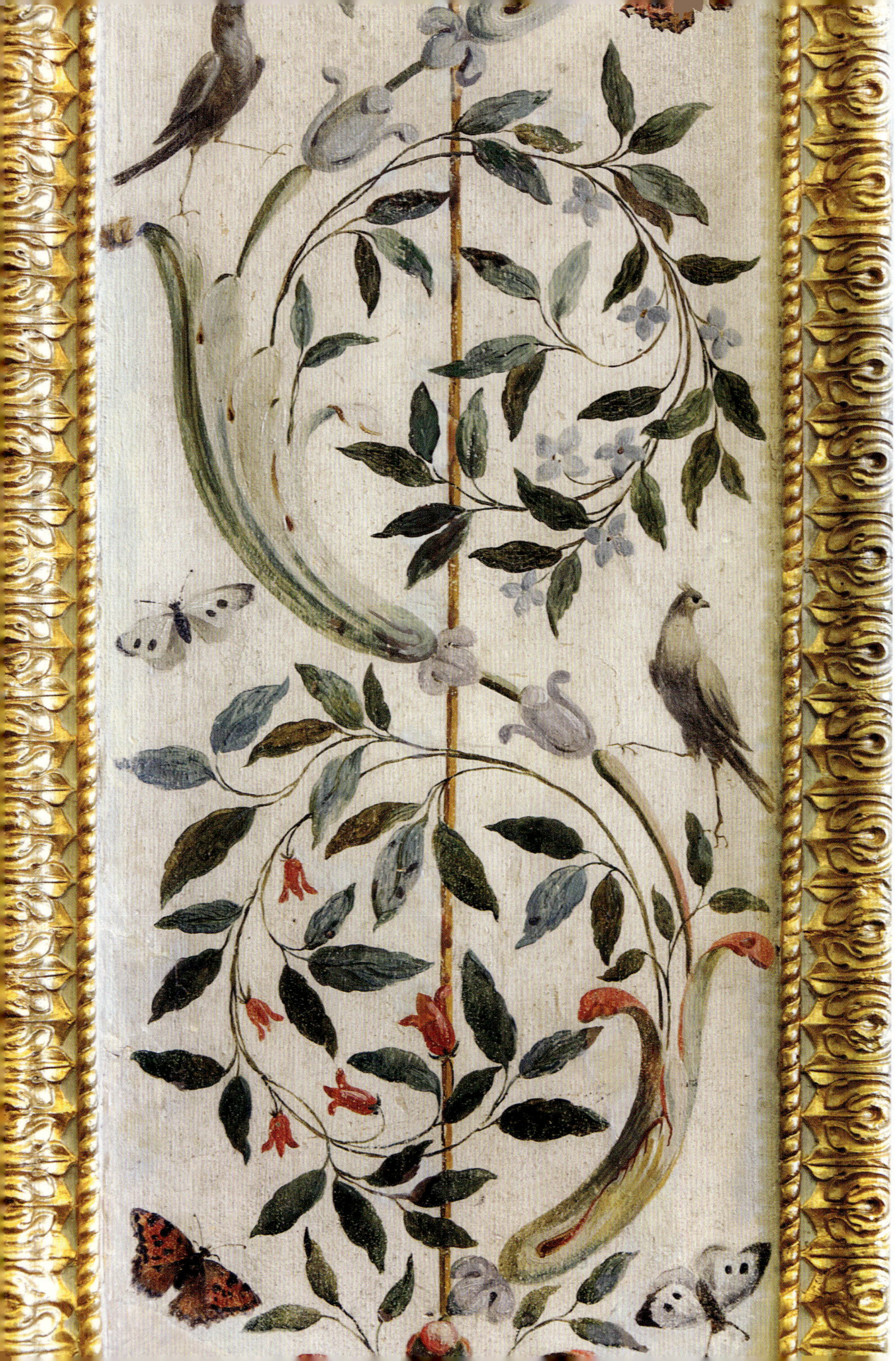

Valdrè's interpretation of classical style shows a lightness of touch and a playful element.

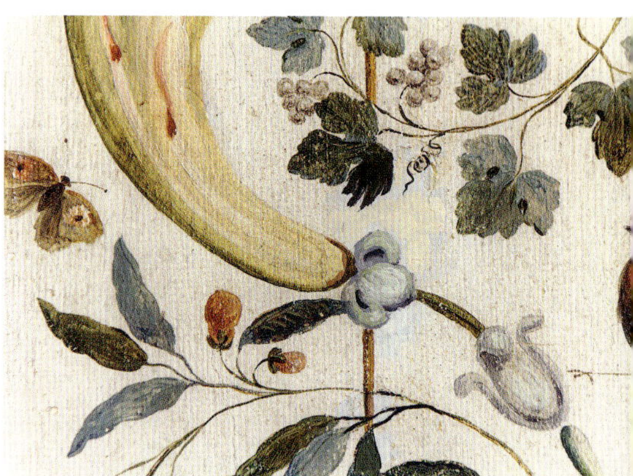

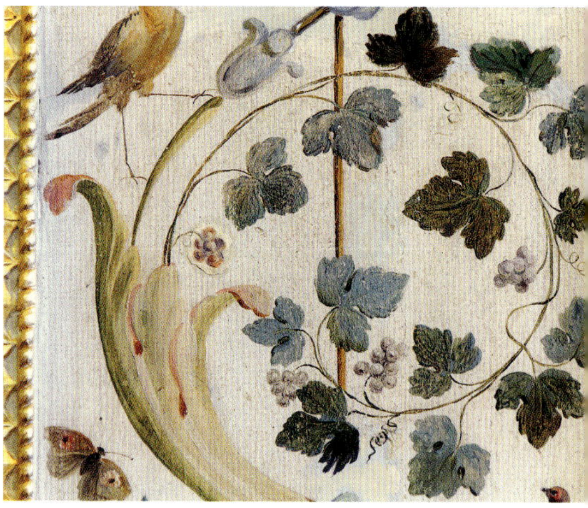

FAR RIGHT
Within the temple of Apollo, the god of music, a lady, possibly representing the music-loving Lady Buckingham, receives a lyre from the god himself.

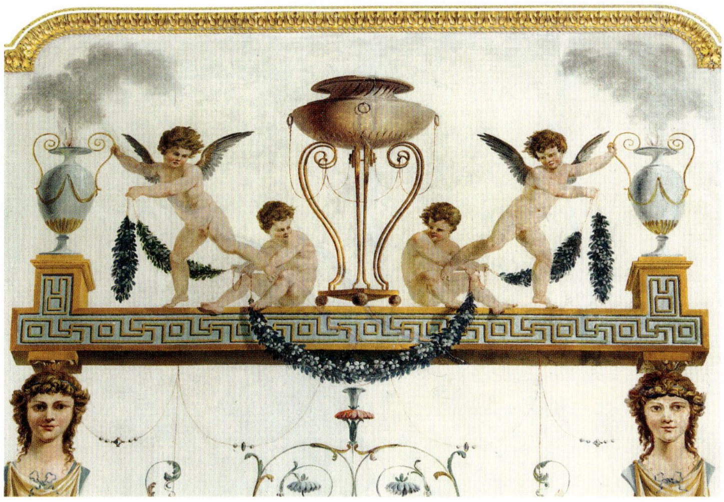

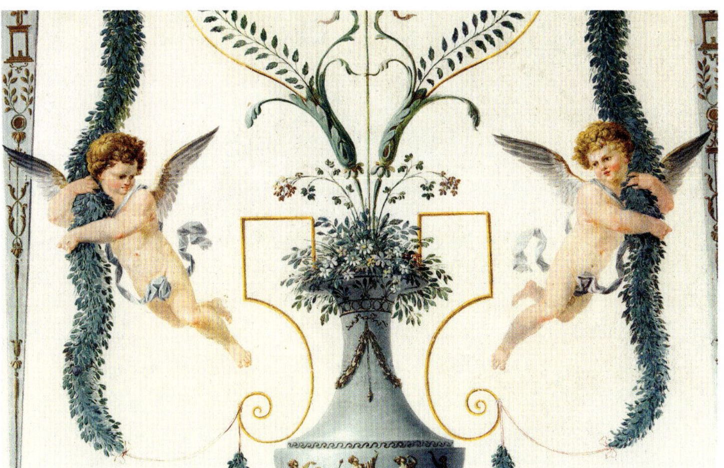

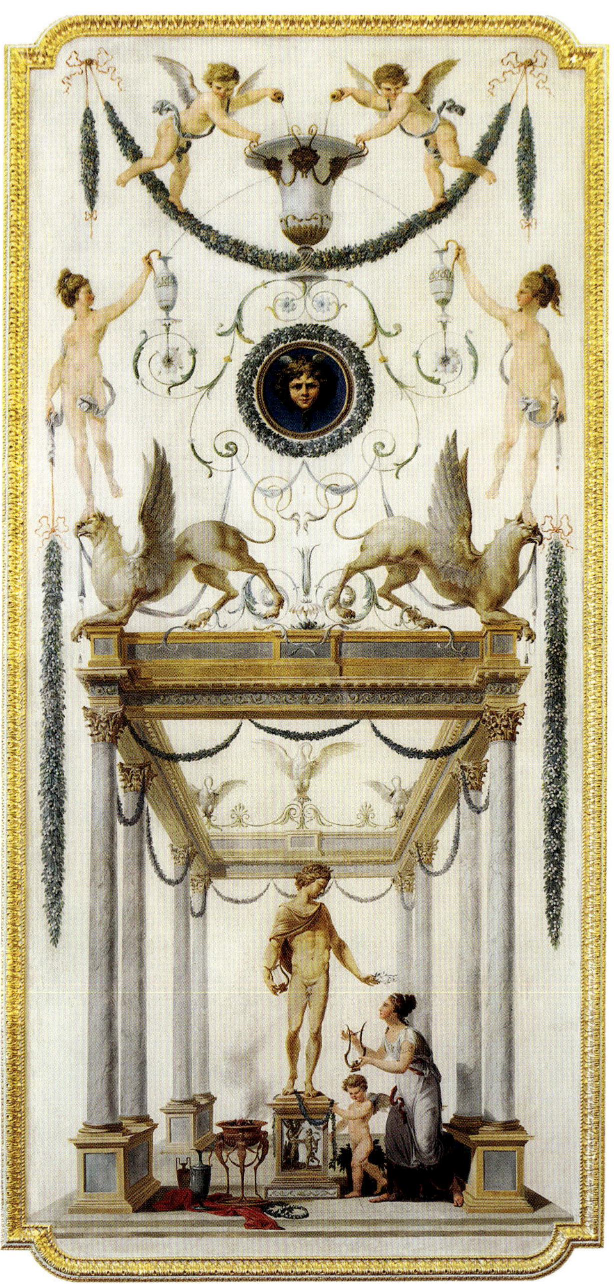

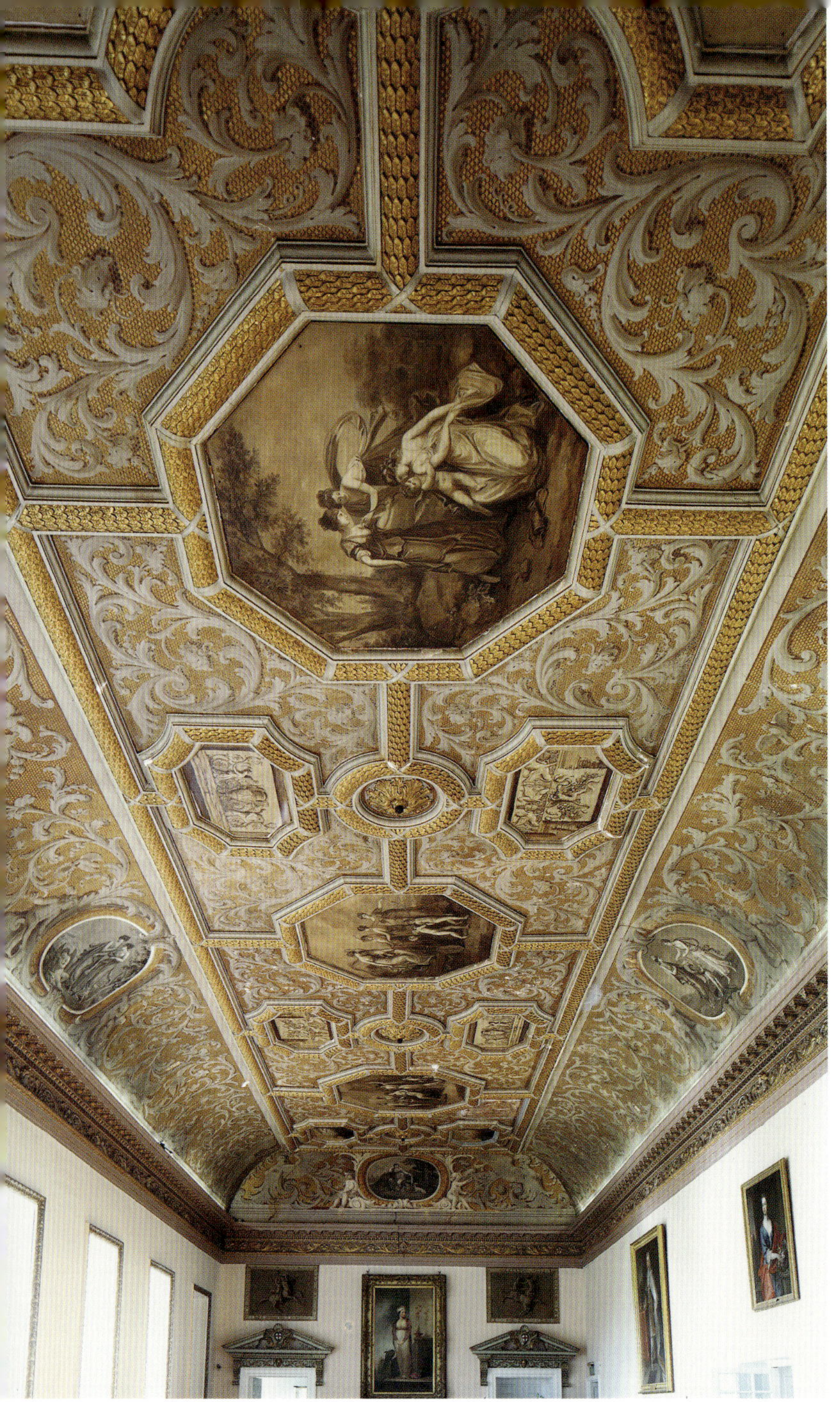

LEFT AND BELOW
Ceiling decoration in the State Dining Room.

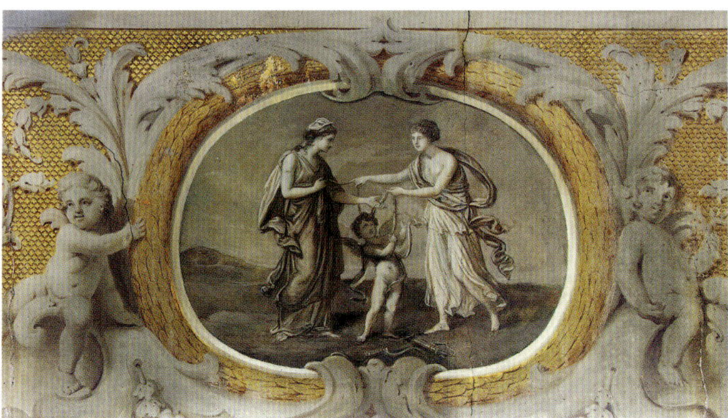

paintings but were also said to have been modelled on Raphael's loggias in the Vatican. At the same time, the State Dining Room was moved to the western side of the House, closer to the kitchens where the State Gallery had been, and its ceiling redecorated.

More intimate spaces were created too and here another great eighteenth-century architect entered the scene. To Sir John Soane is attributed the Gothic Library, built to house the Marquess's collection of Saxon manuscripts, and the Egyptian Hall (or winter entrance), although Soane credited the concept of the latter to the Marquess himself. The Hall was based on the Temple of Dendra, as depicted by Baron Dominique Vivant-Denon, one of 200 artists, scientists and archaeologists who accompanied Napoleon on his Egyptian campaign of 1798. The Baron sketched a remarkable number of monuments, sites and scenes from daily life in Egypt. His book, *Travels in Upper and Lower Egypt*, appeared in England in 1802 and by 1803 Stowe boasted an Egyptian Hall, reflecting the interest in this newly discovered civilisation. Finally, in anticipation of a visit by the book-loving King George III, the Marquess created the Library, with its gilded ceiling, in the place vacated by the State Dining Room.

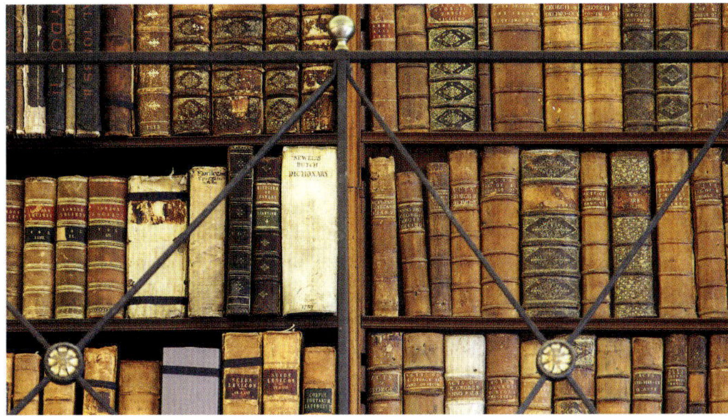

ABOVE
The Library bookshelves, much as the book-loving Marquess would have wished.

RIGHT
Sir John Soane's Gothic Library, built to house Saxon manuscripts, now serves as the Headmaster's Study.

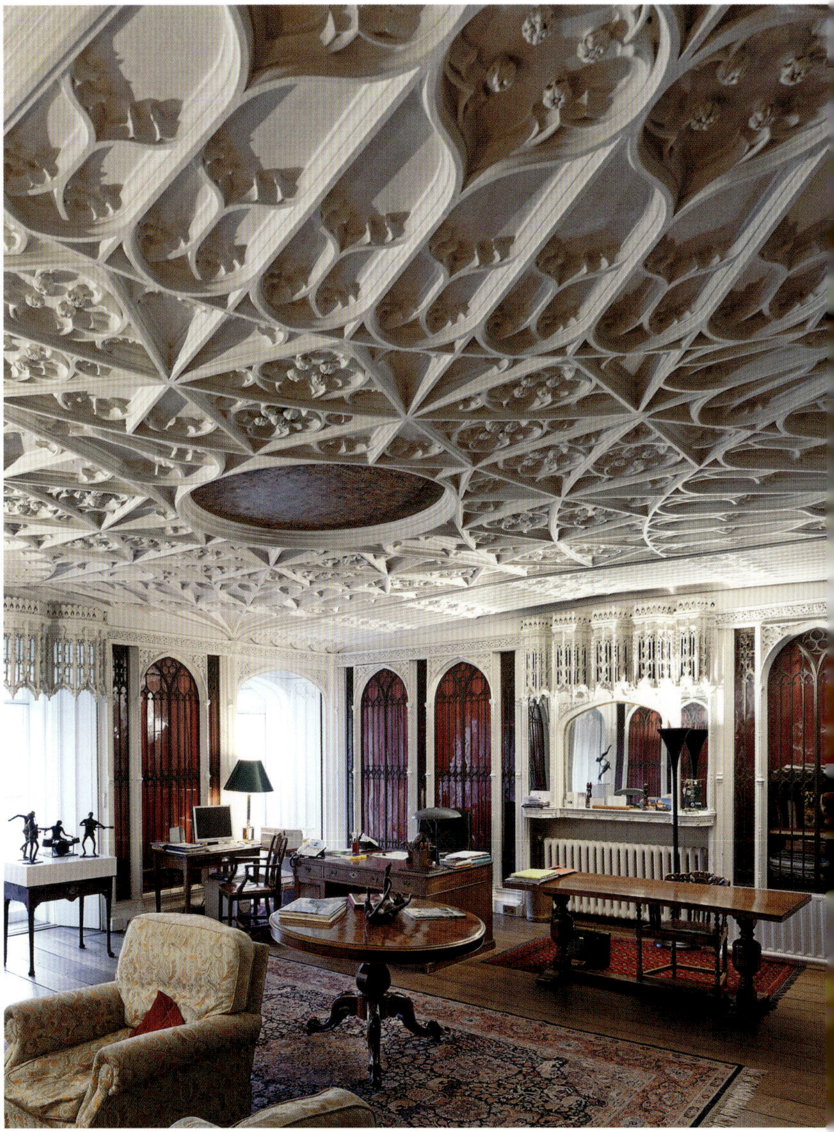

NOTES

1 E.F. Gray, 'The Rise of an English Family: Peter and John Temple to 1603', *Huntington Library Quarterly* (1938), pp. 367–90.
2 Ophelia Field, *The Kit-Cat Club: Friends Who Imagined a Nation* (London, 2008).
3 Christopher Christie, *The British Country House in the Eighteenth Century* (Manchester, 2000), p. 30.

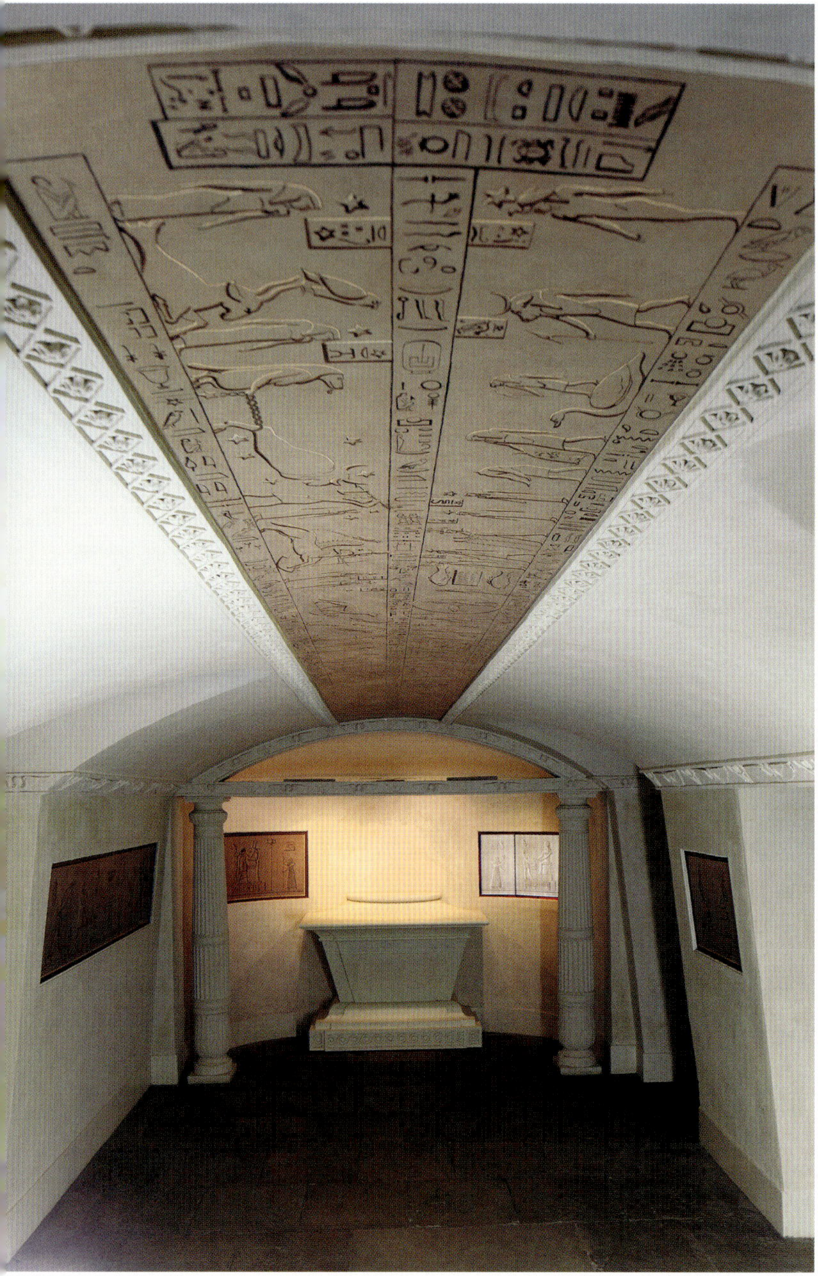

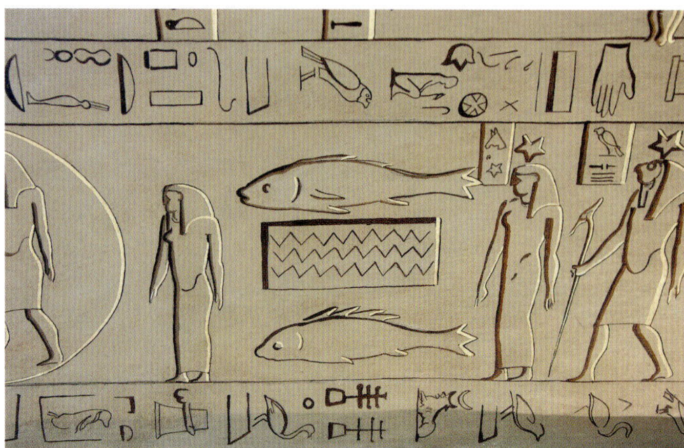

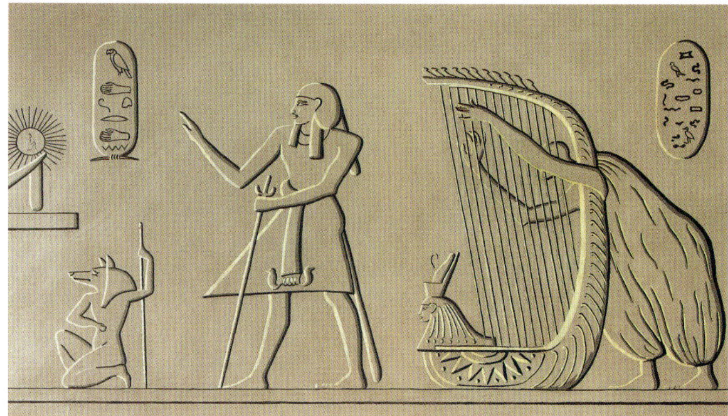

Re-creating the appearance of an Egyptian temple, interpretations of typical wall paintings (above) and the zodiac painted in the portico of the Temple of Dendra (left) feature in the Egyptian Hall.

OPPOSITE
The Library ceiling was gilded with 30,000 leaves of 23.5 carat gold.

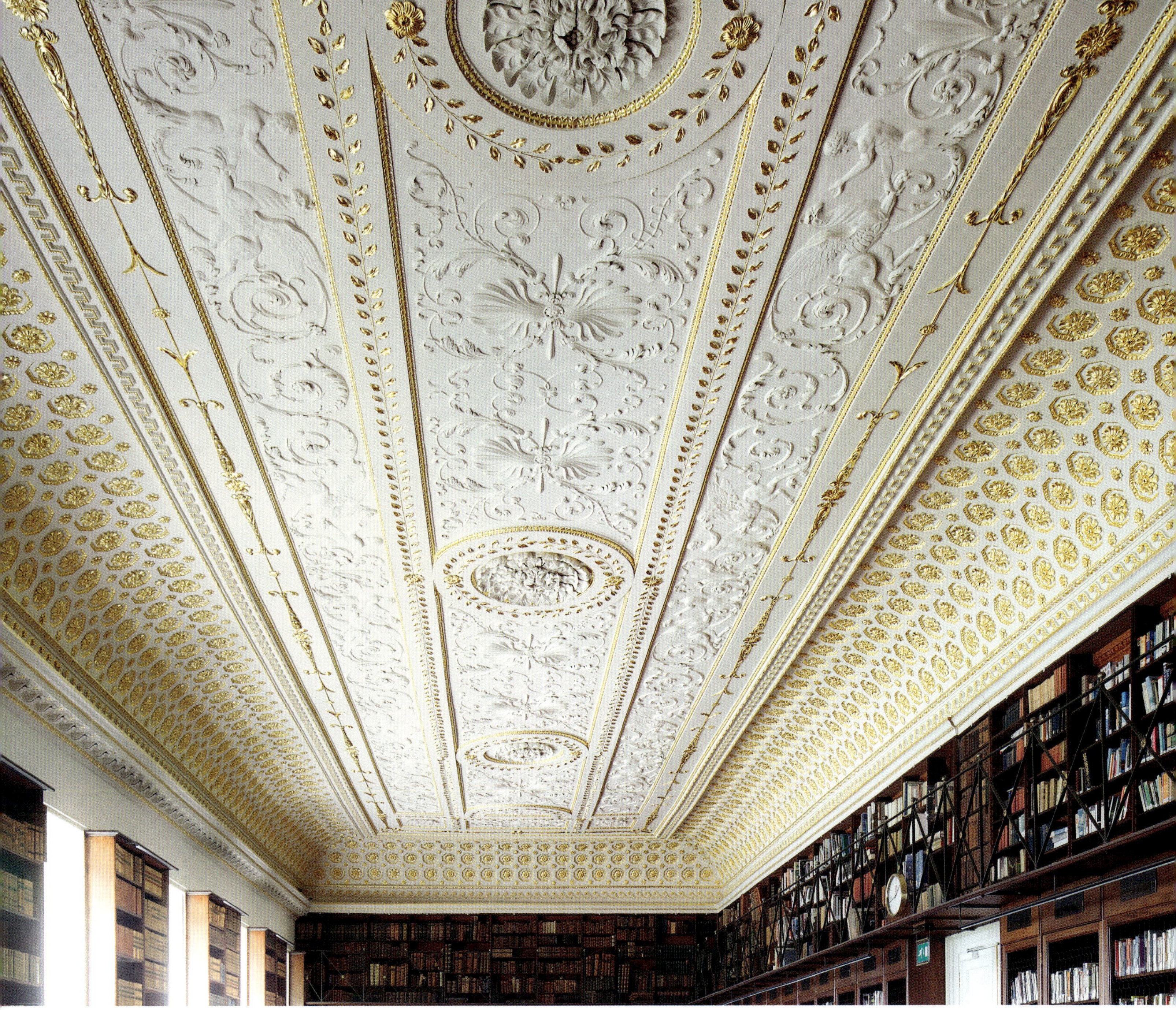

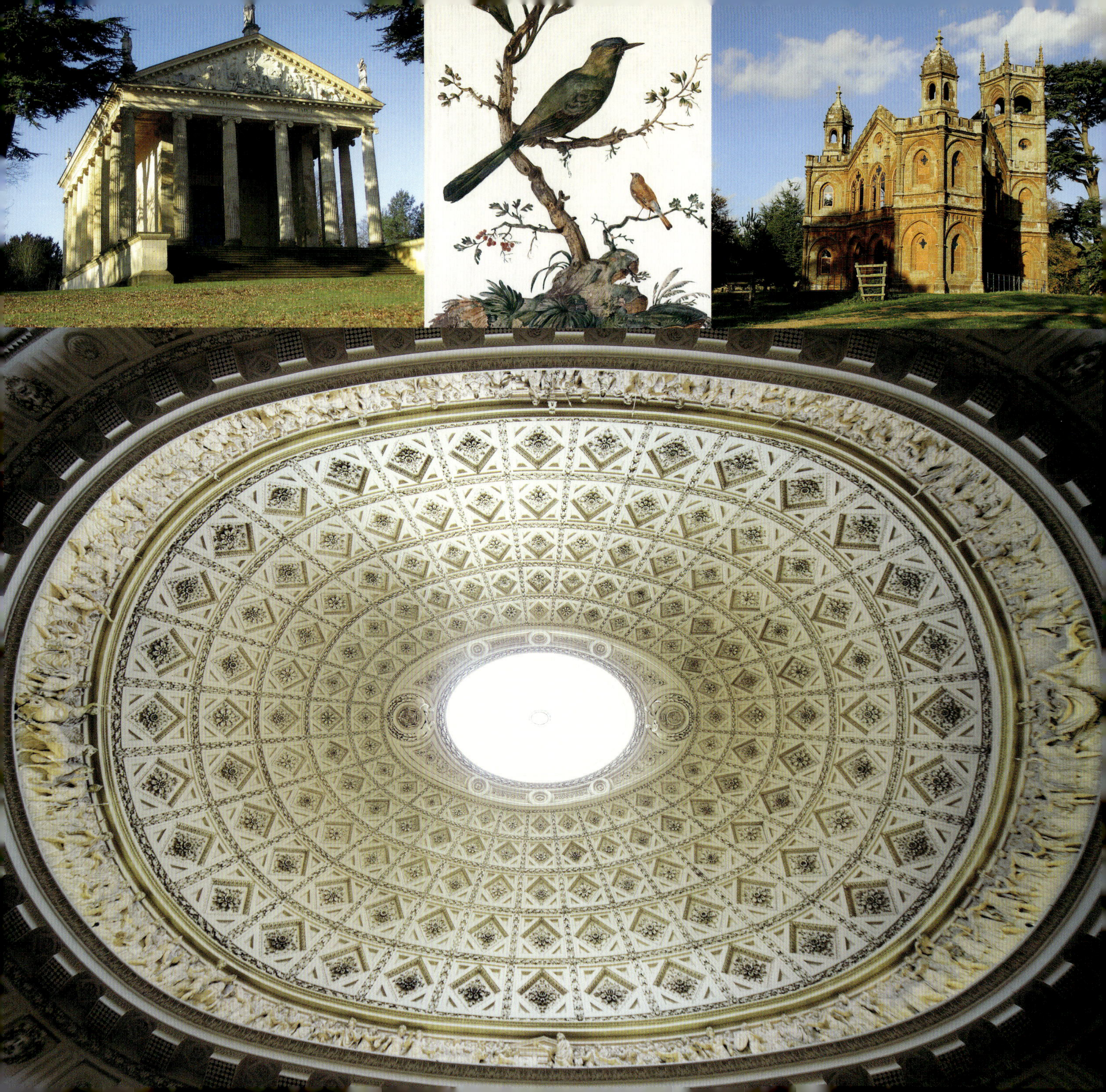

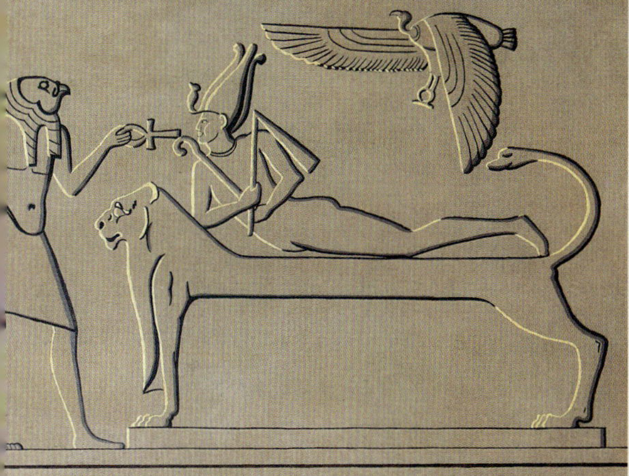

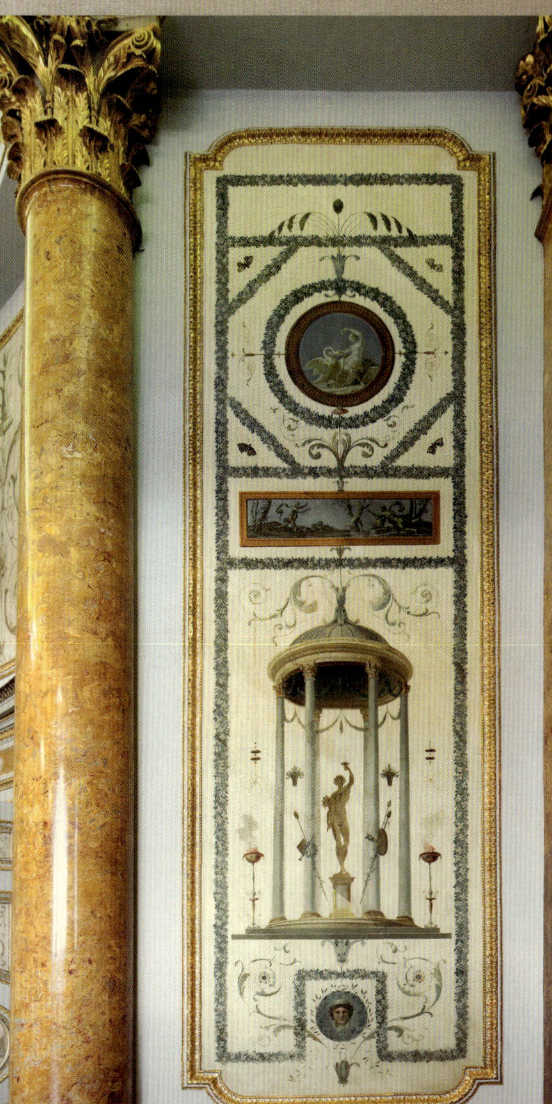

CLOCKWISE FROM TOP LEFT
The Temple of Concord and Victory was influenced by ancient Greece.

French wall covering inspired by Japanese art in one of an intimate suite of rooms (known as the Japanese Room) to the north side of the House.

The Gothic Temple reflects the values of medieval Europe.

Egyptian-style wall paintings adorn the Egyptian Hall.

The State Music Room's wall decorations resemble the style of paintings discovered in Pompeii.

The Marble Saloon's great elliptical domed roof is based on that of the Pantheon in Rome.

CREATIVE INSPIRATIONS AND INFLUENCES

Stowe House is built in the Neo-Classical style. Inspired by archaeology and discoveries from the ancient world, it was in many ways a reaction to the Renaissance and a move away from the more ornate Baroque and Rococo designs. The Grand Tour gave enlightened patrons and their architects an unprecedented view of the monuments of ancient Greece and Rome, which in turn influenced the ways in which they conceived and designed their estates. At Stowe, the House itself draws much from the sixteenth-century Italian architect Andrea Palladio, whose *Four Books on Architecture* (1570) defined and publicised his work. Palladianism was promoted in England by Lord Burlington. His villa at Chiswick House (1727) resembles those by both Palladio in the area around Venice and by British architect Colen Campbell, who designed Mereworth Castle in Kent in 1725.

Within the House, the decoration of the State Music Room owes much to the wall paintings discovered in Pompeii with which the Marquess of Buckingham would have been familiar from his Grand Tour. There are garden buildings inspired by Roman and Grecian temples, columns and triumphal arches, while the Gothic Temple and Gothic Library were influenced by a style found closer to home: European Gothic. The most exciting and exotic discoveries of the age are reflected in the Egyptian Hall, as well as in a room now occupied by the School's Deputy Headmaster on the north side of the House, decorated in the Japanese style, and in a Chinese House in the Landscape Gardens.

In its turn, Stowe influenced design and innovation across the world. Just ouside St Petersburg lie the summer palaces at Tsarskoye Selo (literally Tsar's Village), created by Catherine the Great with parkland and gardens reminiscent of Stowe, complete with a Palladian bridge, rostral column and grottoes. Catherine sent her agent to England and he returned with prints and engravings of the great English country houses, including a large number of Stowe by George Bickham, which are still held in the archive at Tsarskoye Selo. She also commissioned a dinner service from Wedgwood with views of English scenes, on which Stowe features more than any other location. In America, Thomas Jefferson's house at Monticello, built in a Neo-Palladian style, was said to have been influenced by the time that he had spent walking in Stowe's Landscape Gardens, while examples of gardens after the Stowe model are to be found throughout Europe, from Italy to Hungary, and from Poland and Germany to Sweden.

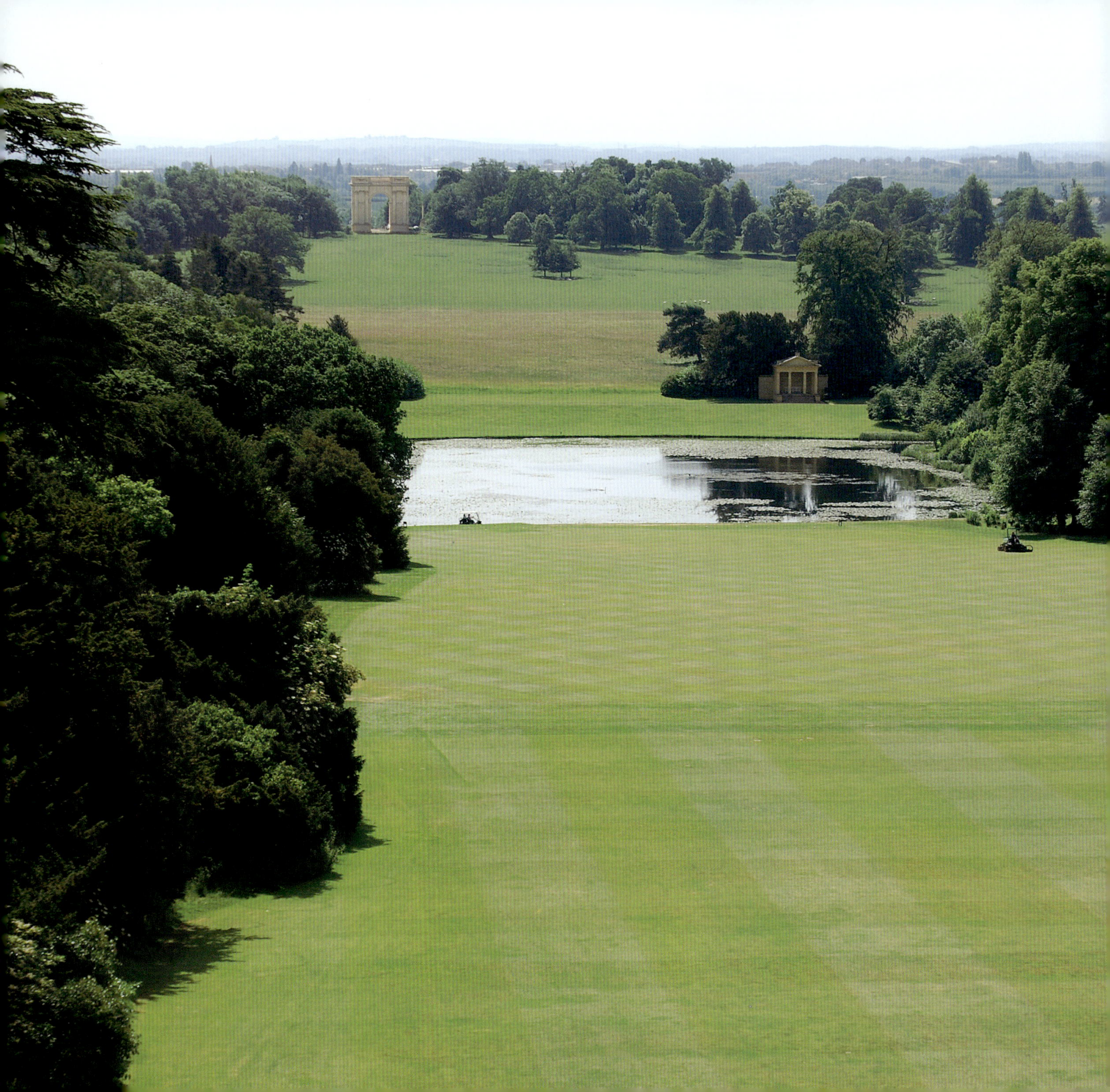

2 EXTRAVAGANCE

Living Beyond Means of Support

George Grenville, 1st Marquess of Buckingham, died in 1813 and was succeeded by his son Richard, but the sinecures and associated income were lost to the family at his death, and it was only a matter of time before Richard's attempts to live in the style of his father exhausted the dwindling resources. He did, however, achieve the family's long-cherished dream of a dukedom and, although it meant a change of politics to the Tory side of the House of Commons, in 1822 he was created 1st Duke of Buckingham and Chandos.

An avid collector and a keen amateur geologist and archaeologist, the 1st Duke added to the family's collections. He also enlarged the gardens at Stowe and acquired further land bordering the Estate, turning part of the Ménagerie into a museum. In 1827, having shut Stowe to save costs, he spent two years on his yacht the *Anna Eliza*, named after his wife Anna Eliza Brydges, a wealthy heiress whom he had married in 1796 and who brought the Chandos name to the family lineage having been betrothed as a child. While on his travels, the Duke painted, sketched and visited the courts and officials of the European countries around which he sailed. He amassed further items and collections along the way and became, allegedly, the fattest man ever carried to the summit of Vesuvius.

Although he added to the contents of the House, the 1st Duke entertained less often than his father, but a notable party was held in February 1818 to celebrate the 21st birthday of his son, Richard Plantagenet Temple-Nugent-Brydges-Chandos-Grenville. Richard acceded to the title in 1839 and might have maintained the Estate had he not inherited his father's extravagance.

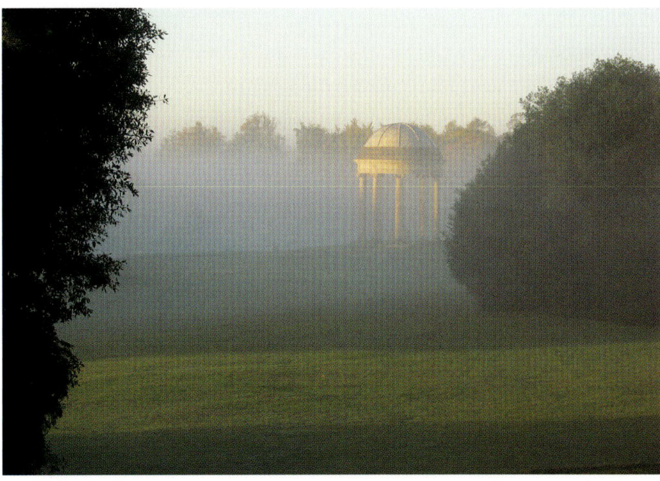

OPPOSITE
A view of the Landscape Gardens from the House.

RIGHT
Vanbrugh's Rotunda emerges from the mist on an autumn morning.

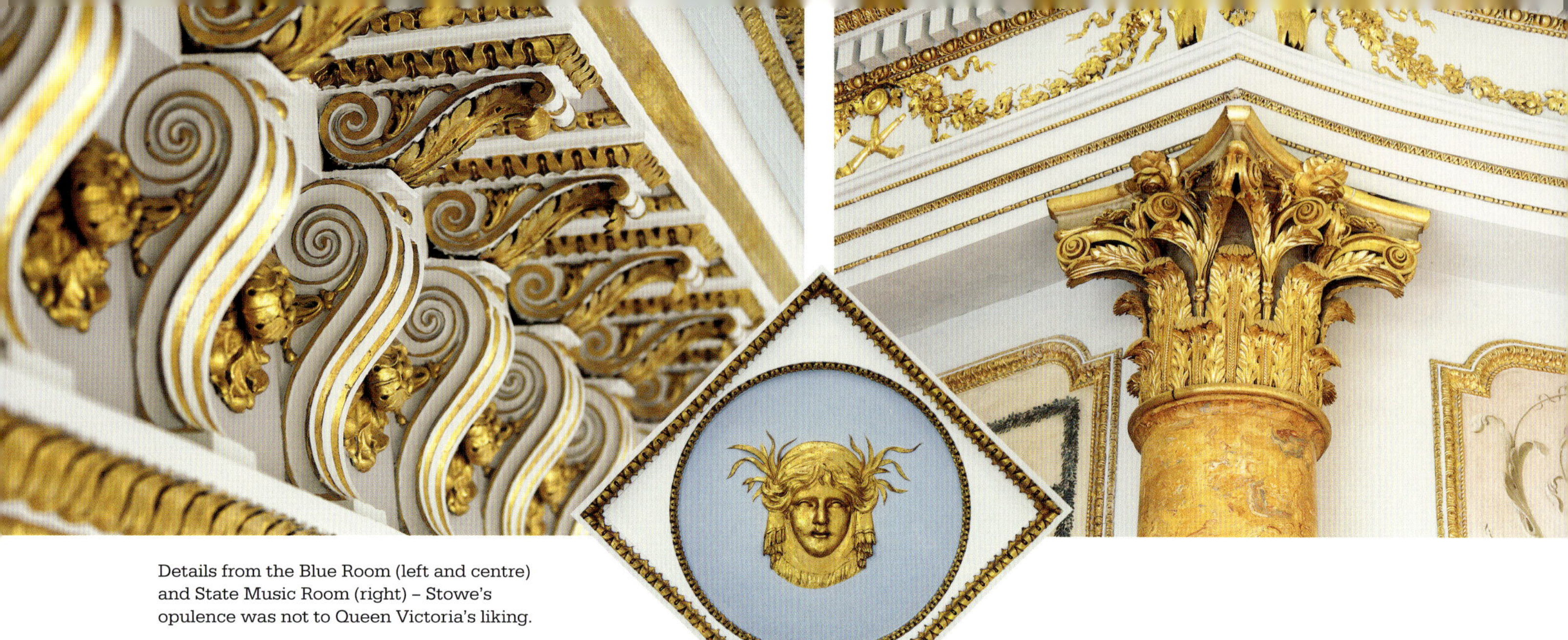

Details from the Blue Room (left and centre) and State Music Room (right) – Stowe's opulence was not to Queen Victoria's liking.

Three Days of Right Royal Entertainment

Even for a house that had seen lavish entertainment, the events of two days in January 1845 must have been extraordinary. Elizabeth George, from nearby Dadford, whose grandfather had been a master carpenter at Stowe in the late eighteenth century, was allowed access to the House and remarked on what she saw – and heard – about the royal visit. She records the expense to which the 2nd Duke committed in order to impress Queen Victoria and Prince Albert, noting that virtually every part of the House had been refurnished and decorated. She reports that the Queen commented, 'I am sure I have no such splendid apartments in either of my palaces', and suggests that she would have been far happier with more simple furnishings.[4] Elizabeth's own reflection was that the House was overcrowded and took on the appearance of a large furniture warehouse, and she notes the head housemaid having heard the Queen remark that she had previously turned down an offer to purchase the carpet in her bedroom as she had found it too costly.

A contemporary engraving shows the mounted ranks of the Buckinghamshire Yeomanry formed up facing the House, welcoming a procession of carriages, while various others on foot line the semi-circular colonnades that embrace the North Front. The Yeomanry were the escorting troops for Queen Victoria and Prince Albert, whose train had stopped en route to Chatsworth to enable them to see Stowe at the invitation of the Duke. Tenants and labourers gathered on the approaches to the Estate, while whole rooms in the House were redecorated in honour of the royal couple. Orchestras and police had even been drafted in from London. Victoria and Albert stayed for two nights and the former State Dressing Room and State Bedchamber in which they slept, now named the Green and Victoria Rooms at the eastern end of the House, are still in use today as boys' boarding accommodation. A watercolour by Joseph Nash shows the Queen sitting amidst the splendour of the State Drawing Room (now known as the Temple Room).

The Beginning of the End

Unfortunately, the 2nd Duke could ill afford this opulent show of hospitality. He engaged in some questionable financial practices to enable repairs and further work on the Estate and, in August 1847, the bailiffs arrived, acting for his creditors. They seized his effects and, while he fled

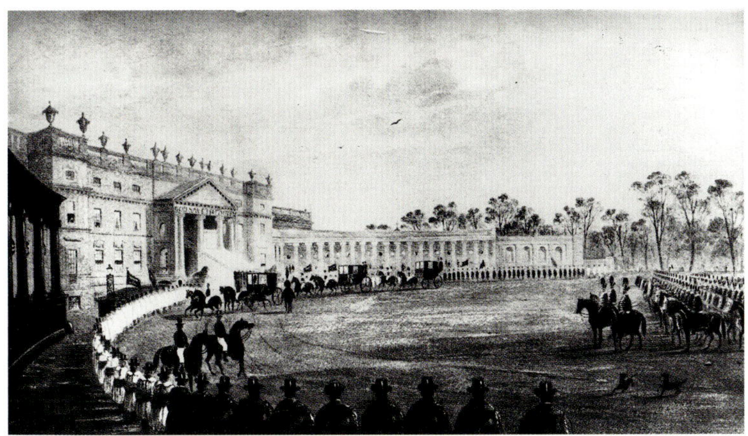

Queen Victoria arriving at the North Front, welcomed by the Yeomanry, 1845.

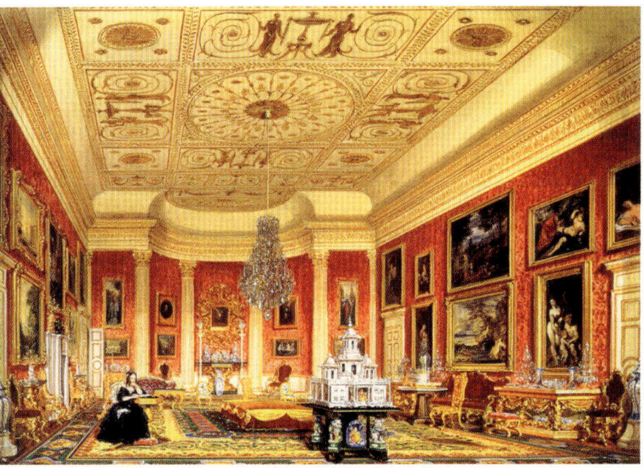

A watercolour by Joseph Nash showing a lady in black, perhaps meant to represent Queen Victoria, in the State Drawing Room, 1845.

Stowe, his affairs were taken over by his son Chandos, the 3rd Duke, and a board of trustees. In May 1848 a 40-day sale administered by Christie's saw the House cleared of the accumulated treasures and in *The Times* of 14 August 1848 Thomas Babington Macaulay wrote:

> During the past week the British public has been admitted to a spectacle of a painfully interesting and gravely historical import. One of the most splendid abodes of our almost regal aristocracy has thrown open its portals to an endless succession of visitors ... not to enjoy the hospitality of the lord, or to congratulate him on his countless treasures of art, but to see an ancient family ruined, their place marked for destruction, and its contents scattered to the four winds of Heaven. ... the Most Noble and Puissant Prince, his Grace the Duke of Buckingham and Chandos, is at this moment an absolutely ruined and desolate man. ... Stowe is no more.

The 3rd Duke managed to recover the situation and set up a programme that today would be called an 'austerity' approach, laying off staff and closing down buildings. He made some changes to the House, most notably the Blue Room, Stowe's only interior to be presented in the Victorian style. There is no disguising the surprise in Benjamin Disraeli's commentary following the 3rd Duke's return in 1865: 'the flag flies once again over Stowe, which no one expected'.[5]

When he died in 1889, the 3rd Duke left no male heir and the dukedom died with him 67 years after it had been created. His eldest daughter, Mary, Lady Morgan-Grenville, inherited the title Lady Kinloss. Having no use for the House, she considered selling it but let it briefly to the exiled claimant to the French throne, the Comte de Paris. The Comte died at Stowe having spent five years there. During this time the Chapel was moved from its former location (shown on the Plan as the Old Chapel), where some of the original wood panelling can still be seen, to the larger room next door so that it could enjoy the traditional east–west orientation as opposed to north–south. Both rooms now serve as house common rooms for pupils, the name Paris Room commemorating the Comte's association with Stowe.

Sadly, Lady Kinloss's eldest son Richard, Master of Kinloss, was killed in action during the First World War, aged 27. Educated at Eton and the Royal Military Academy,

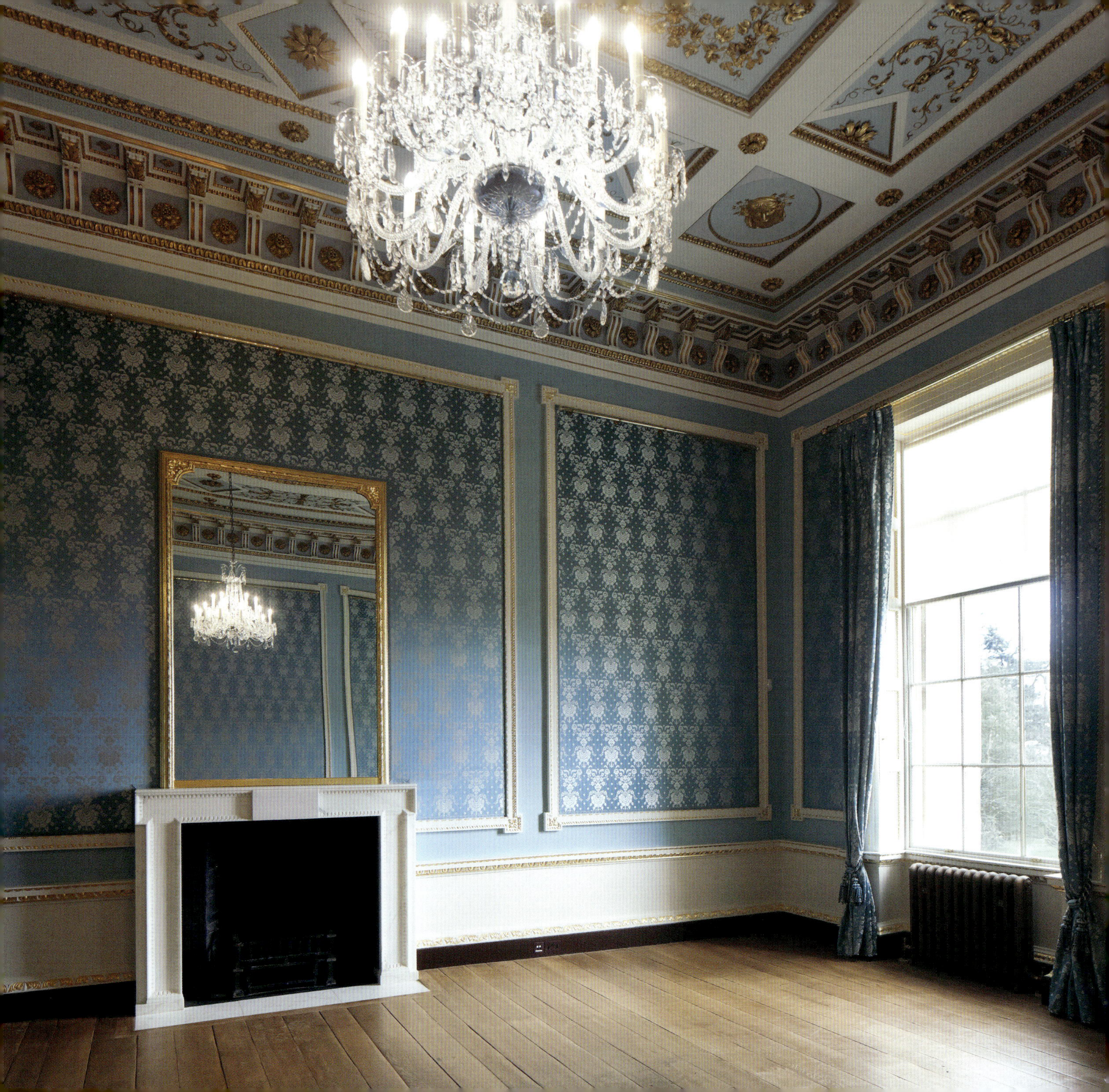

OPPOSITE
The refurbished Blue Room in 2015.

BELOW
Bespoke silk curtains and tie-backs reflect Victorian style in the beautifully restored Blue Room.

RIGHT
Still much as it would have appeared in the 1860s, the Blue Room photographed in 1921.

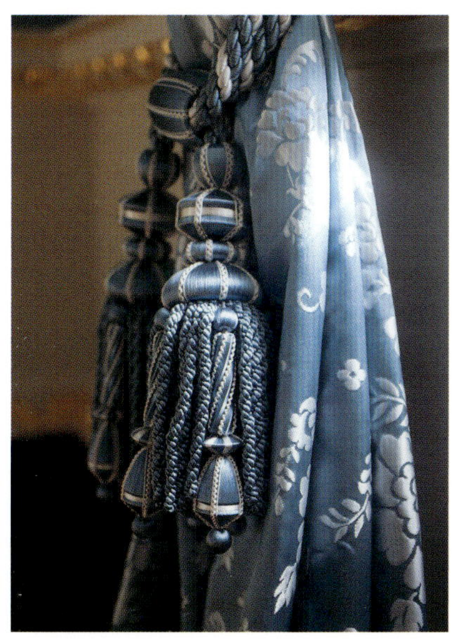

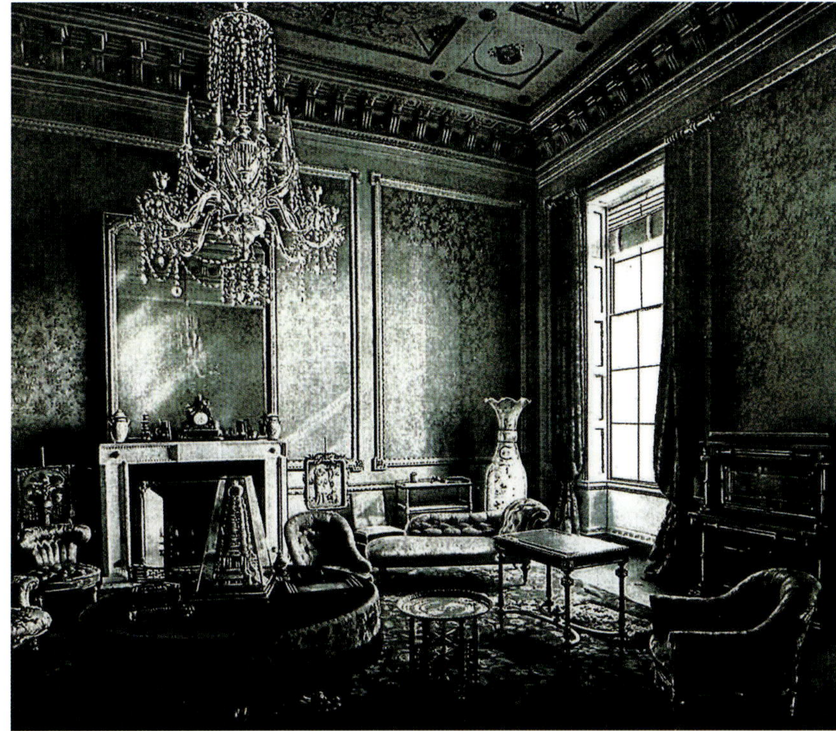

Sandhurst, he had joined the 1st Battalion of the Rifle Brigade on 24 January 1906 and went to France with the British Expeditionary Force. Twice mentioned in despatches for bravery, he was recommended for the Distinguished Service Order but, having given his Christmas leave to a colleague in whose place he remained at the front, he was killed in an attack on German House in Ploegsteert Wood on 19 December 1914. With him, Stowe's story as a private house died: Lady Kinloss could not maintain the Estate and Richard's younger brother, the Reverend Louis Grenville, put Stowe on the market in 1921. The purchaser, Mr Harry Shaw, had intended to present the House to the nation but he was unable to raise sufficient funds to ensure its upkeep and so it was sold again in 1922, this time to the Reverend Percy Warrington, acting on behalf of a group founding new independent schools. Richard's selfless action, therefore, laid the foundation for re-birth when in 1923, nine years after his death, new life was breathed into the building and a very different cast entered the stage at the opening of Stowe School.

NOTES

4 'The Journal of Elizabeth George of Dadford', in *Recollections of Nineteenth-Century Buckinghamshire* (Buckinghamshire Record Society, 1998), pp. 67–122.

5 Robert Blake, *Disraeli* (London, 1996), p. 494.

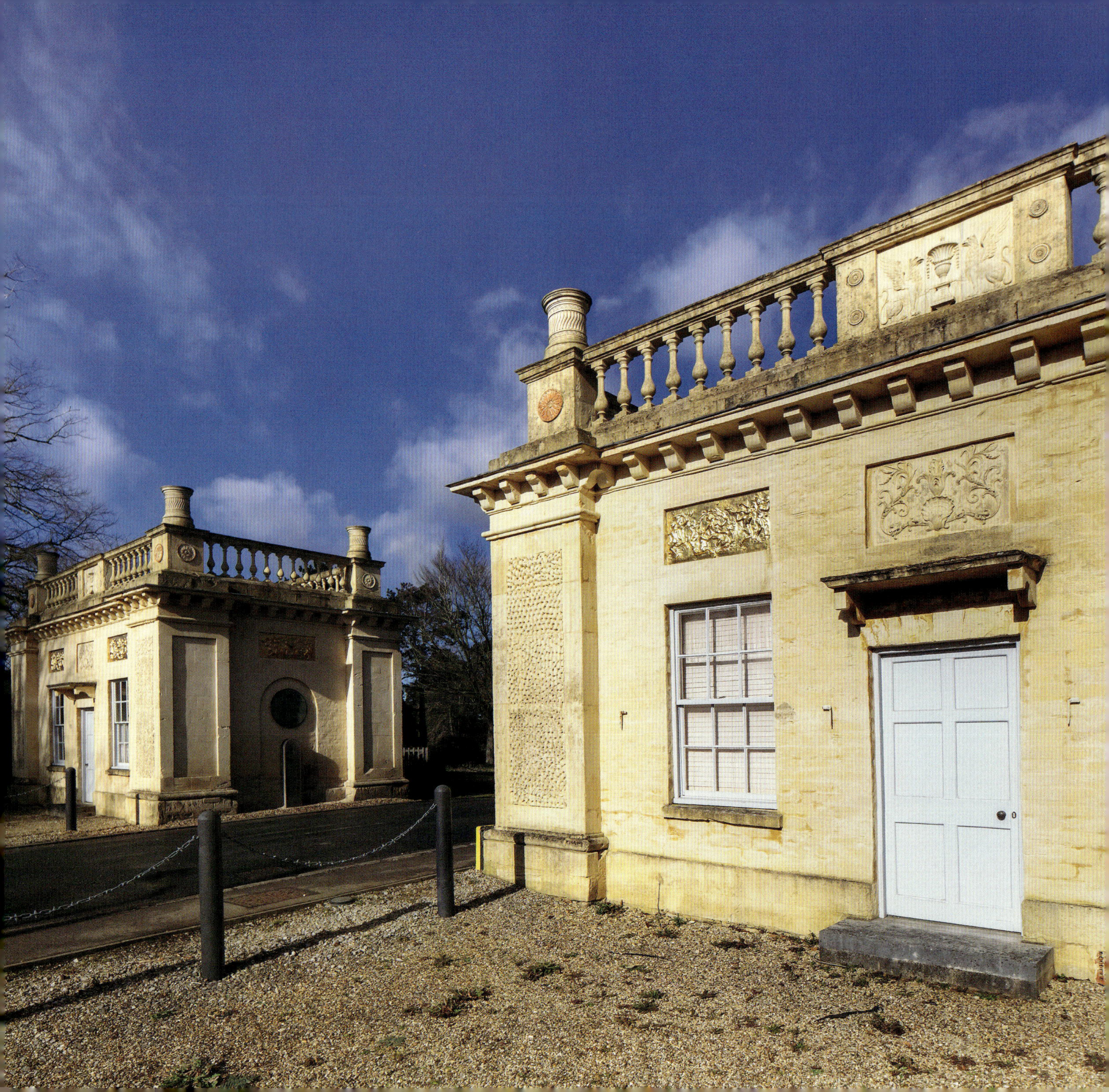

3 RESCUE

A Symbol

Outside the town of Buckingham, two miles south of Stowe House, stand two lodges designed by Vicenzo Valdrè, architect of the Ménagerie and the artist responsible for the State Music Room. On the wall of the western lodge there is a plaque that bears witness to a gift that typifies Stowe's development as a seat of learning and influence. An inscription in Latin reads: '1924. That the voice of their murmuring leaves might not be silenced, Etonians redeemed these trees and offered them to the new-born school with this prayer: that it stand fast and stand first. July 17th'. It records the purchase and subsequent gift to Stowe School of Stowe Avenue, the majestic approach that leads towards the House from Buckingham. Originally purchased by the School's first architect, Sir Clough Williams-Ellis, to prevent it from becoming a 'ribbon development' of the town, the Avenue is symbolic of the plight of the whole Estate from 1921, when it was put up for sale. The Avenue can be seen as a christening present to the School from one of its illustrious forebears.

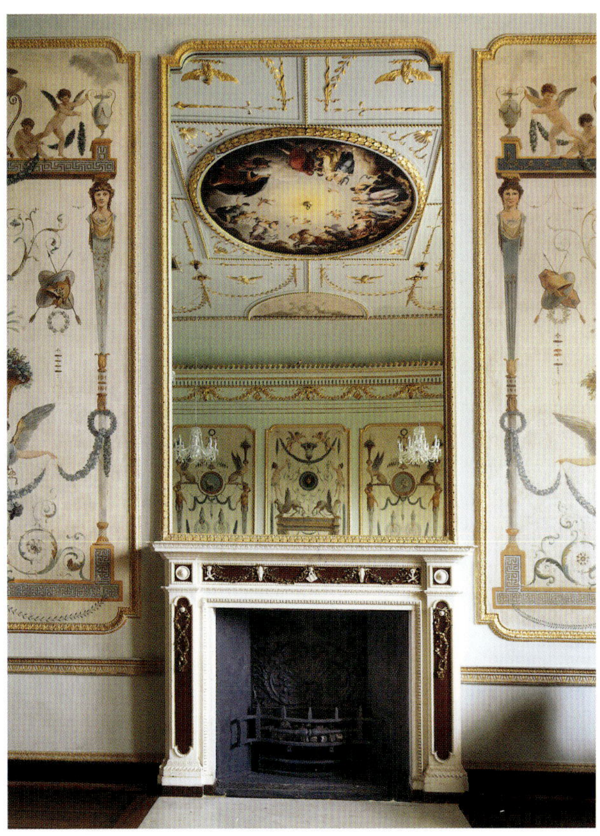

OPPOSITE
The Buckingham lodges by Vicenzo Valdrè.

RIGHT
Also by Valdrè, the *Dance of the Hours* is reflected in the mirror of his great work, the State Music Room.

RIGHT
The plaque on the western Buckingham lodge records Eton College's gift of Stowe Avenue to the newly created Stowe School.

FAR RIGHT
Stowe Avenue with the House in the distance.

BOTTOM RIGHT
The South Front at night.

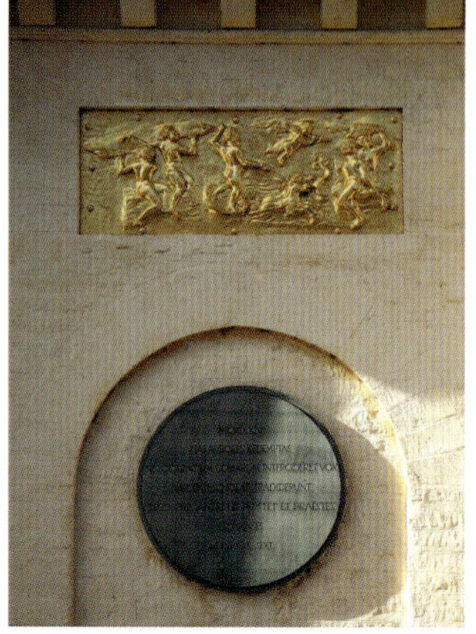

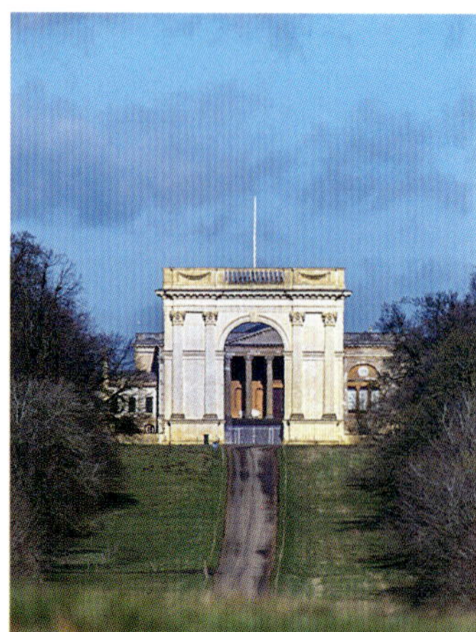

A Challenge of Some Magnitude

Clough Williams-Ellis, the architect of Portmeirion in North Wales, had already campaigned for town and regional planning in a number of cities when he was invited to write an article on Stowe, its past and present state, for *The Spectator.* This article led to him being invited to become the architect charged with transforming the site into a Public School that would maintain the greatest traditions of the Enlightenment. In his own words, Williams-Ellis set about the work,

> with the greatest enthusiasm for here, as I knew, was exemplified classical domestic architecture on the grandest scale ... All the outcome of some two centuries of evolution under a succession of architects and landscapists of the highest distinction working for appreciative patrons who seemed ever ready to launch out on new embellishments, no matter what the cost.[6]

The task facing Williams-Ellis was very different from that of his predecessors, all of whom had been engaged to embellish or update the House in line with changing tastes, lifestyles and ambitions. To him fell a true transformation of the building: one that would guarantee its survival, not just as a priceless example of graceful and refined architecture but also as a seat of creativity, learning and endeavour:

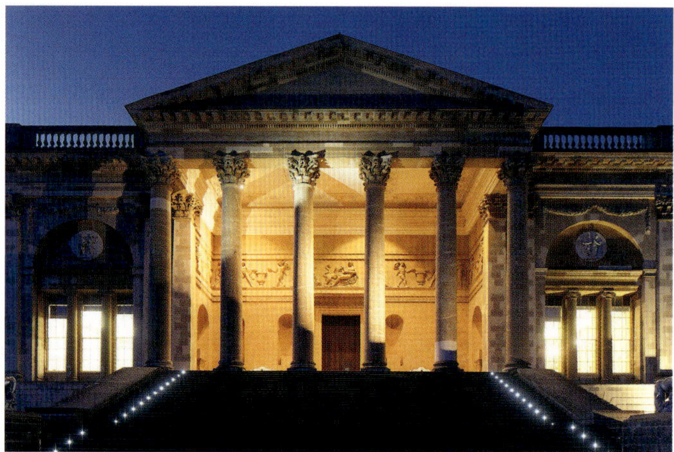

> So almost at once there I was with this great echoing long-neglected palace of four hundred rooms to deal with ... *sans* water supply, *sans* drains, heating, lighting or even adequate maintenance. Somehow the huge building had to be transformed into a reasonably functioning school for – to start with – 200 boys in four separate 'houses' within the fabric. All this was to be done in a matter of months and the number to be accommodated was to be increased two- or threefold later on.[7]

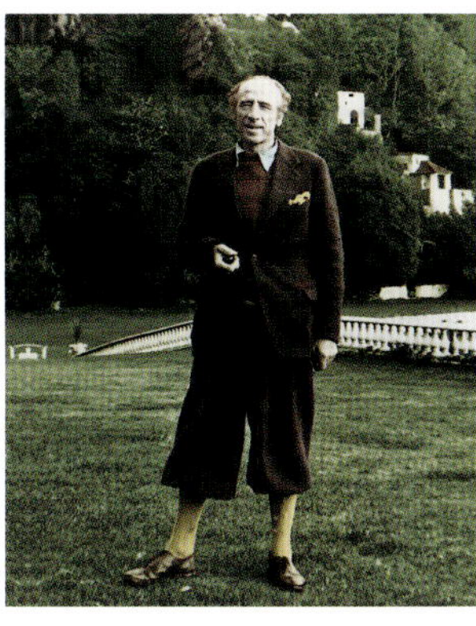

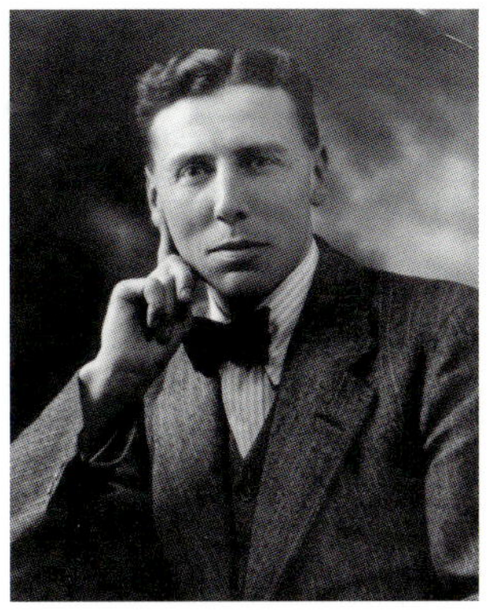

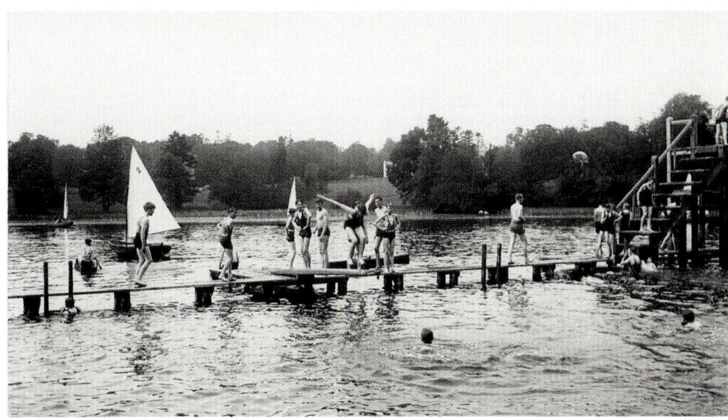

Cost, never an issue for the Temple-Grenvilles, was to be a watchword for Williams-Ellis as he set about creating classrooms and dormitories in the State Rooms and planning new buildings within an historic setting of such significance. Astonishingly, for a House with over 400 rooms, there was only one fitted bathroom. The bath had to be filled by hand from the water that drained from the roof. Over 30 miles of pipes and electrical wiring were installed in the House and a pipe that had originally transported freshly brewed beer from the brewery to the cellars was converted into an oil pipe to heat the water for 60 new baths and 120 washbasins.

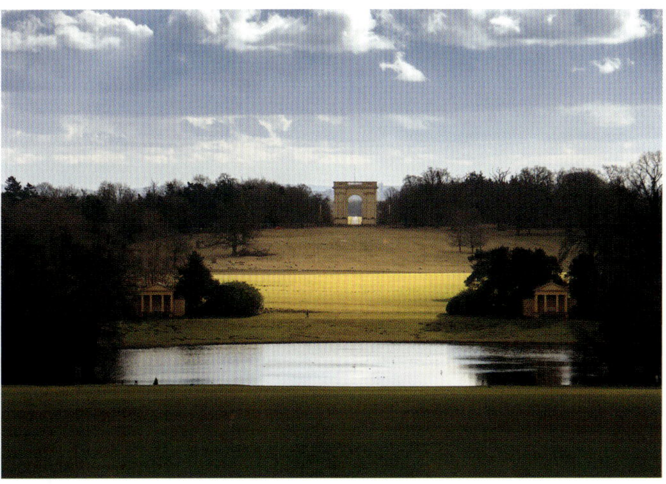

An Enlightened Approach

Clough Williams-Ellis records the support that he enjoyed from the School's first Headmaster, J.F. Roxburgh, known universally as 'JF', who, perhaps more than anyone else, represented that essential link in enlightened thinking from Stowe's origins to its new purpose. In his first public speech as Headmaster, Roxburgh highlighted his ideas on modernising, liberalising and humanising the approach of a boarding school, adding that anyone who had ever 'looked up one of our long green valleys at the great South Front of Stowe in the light of a spring day' would understand that 'Every boy who goes out from Stowe will know beauty when he sees it all the rest of his life'.[8]

TOP LEFT
Clough Williams-Ellis in 1936 on the lawn at Portmeirion, the village he built on the coast of Snowdonia from 1925 to 1973.

TOP CENTRE
J.F. Roxburgh, the School's first Headmaster.

TOP RIGHT
Bathing Pool, Eleven-Acre Lake, 1920s.

ABOVE
Stowe's long green valleys are a sign of enduring beauty.

BELOW
Clough Williams-Ellis extended the School to the west, building a classroom block onto the former Orangery.

BOTTOM
The Chapel by Sir Robert Lorimer.

BELOW RIGHT
John Bickerdike's 'Jazz Age' or 'Utility Lions' stood guard over the South Front for over 90 years until the return of the original Medici lions, when the former were moved to outside the School's Chapel.

OPPOSITE
The majestic South Front.

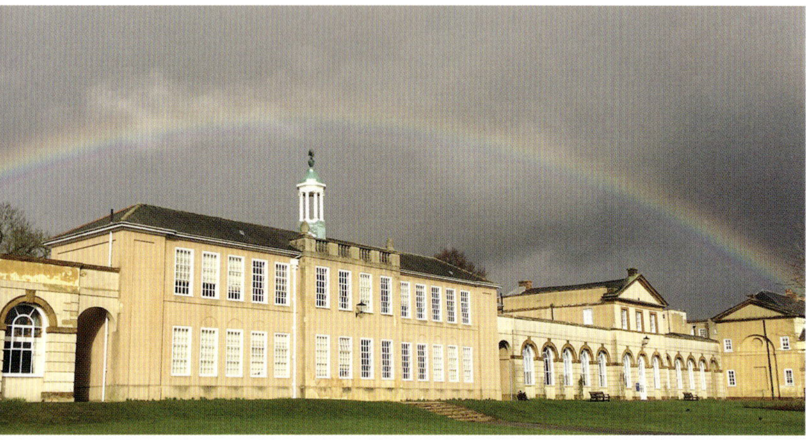

As well as adapting existing buildings, Williams-Ellis added to the distinguished architecture on the site, extending the line of the Orangery to the west. At a suitable distance from the Orangery, he planned a mirror image of the building, joining this copy to the original with a more functional-looking block. Together, the three buildings now form an elegant classroom range, enclosing the north side of Chapel Court, the east and west sides of which are filled respectively by the former office wing of the House and the Chapel (by Sir Robert Lorimer). On the South Front, Williams-Ellis replaced the magnificent Medici lions that had been sold in 1922 with, in his words, 'plausible understudies' or 'Utility Lions', cast in concrete by John Bickerdike. The recovery in 2013 of the originals and the

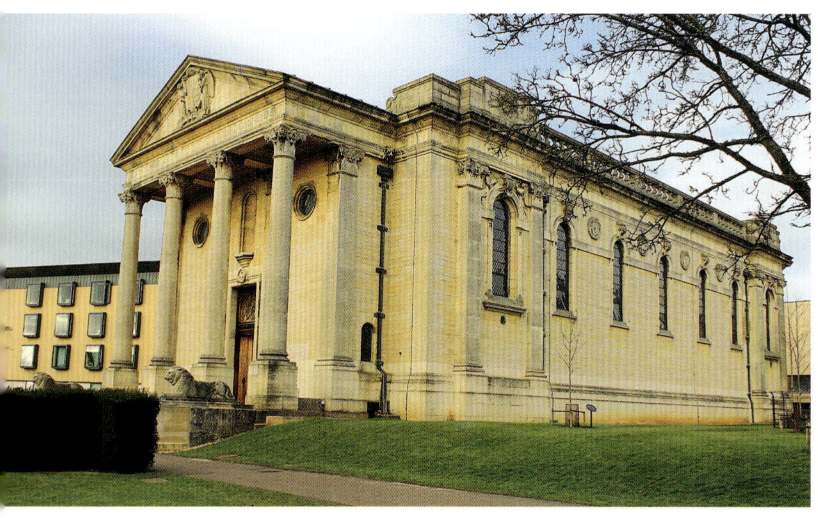

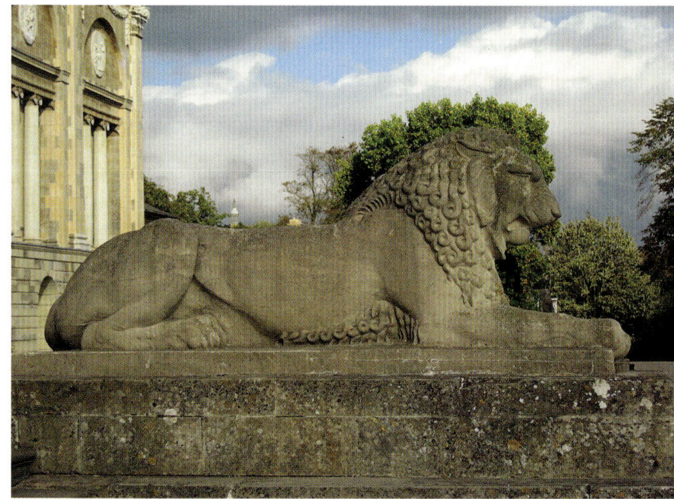

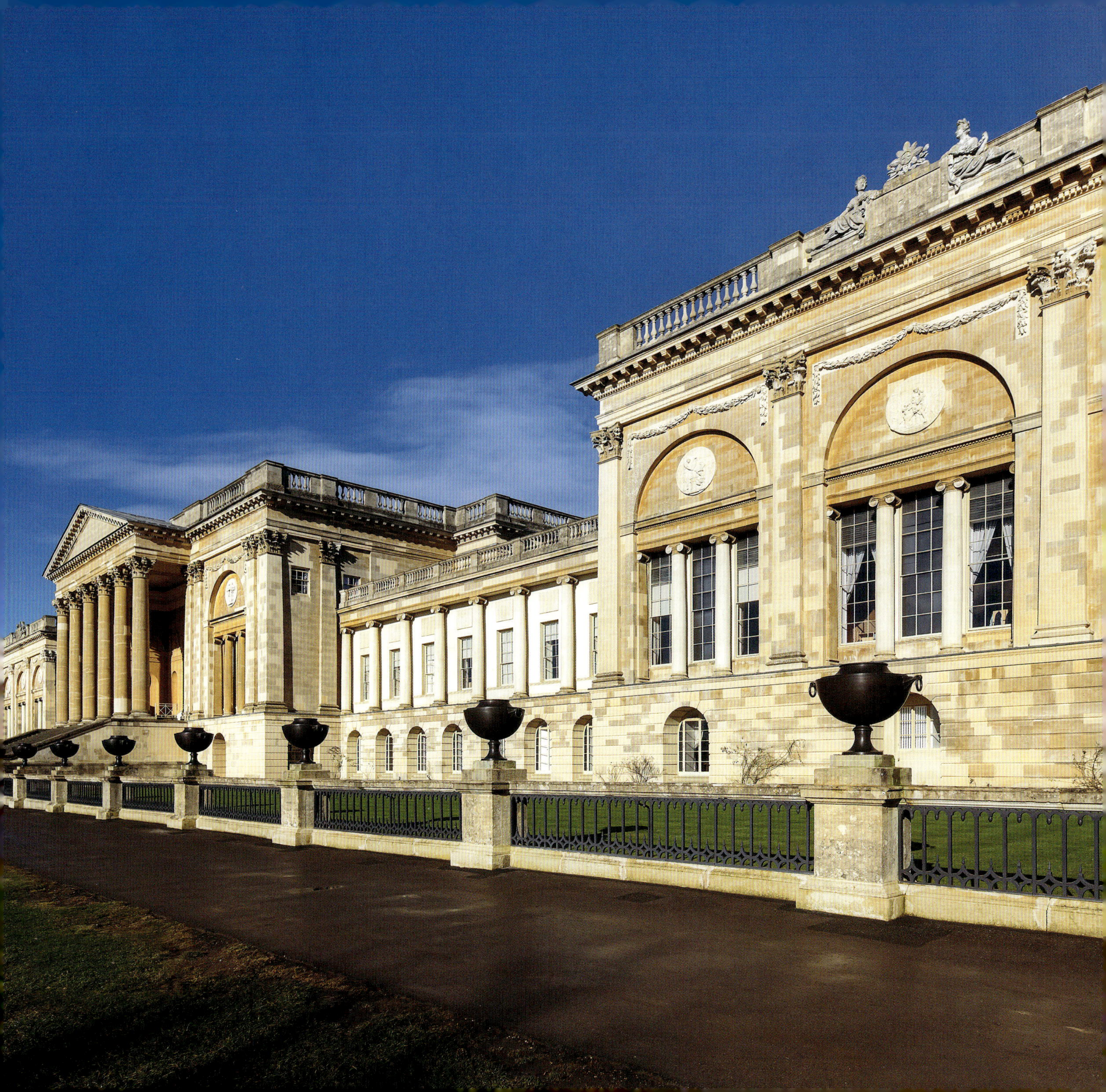

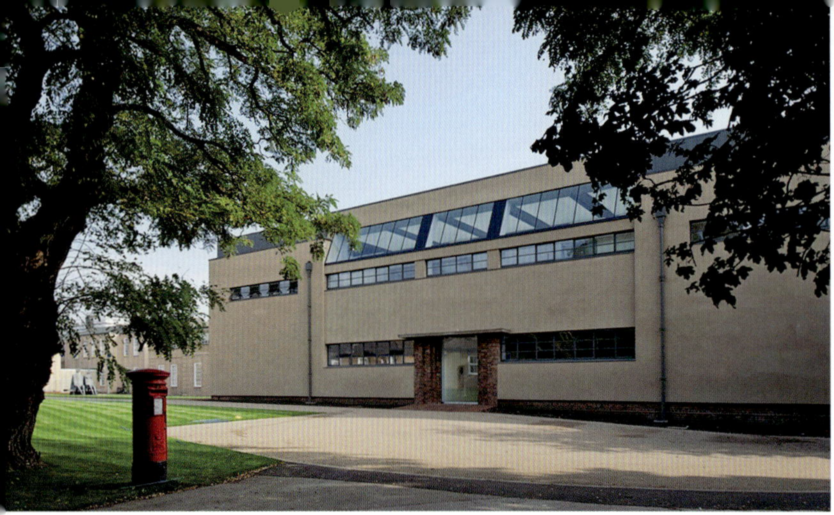

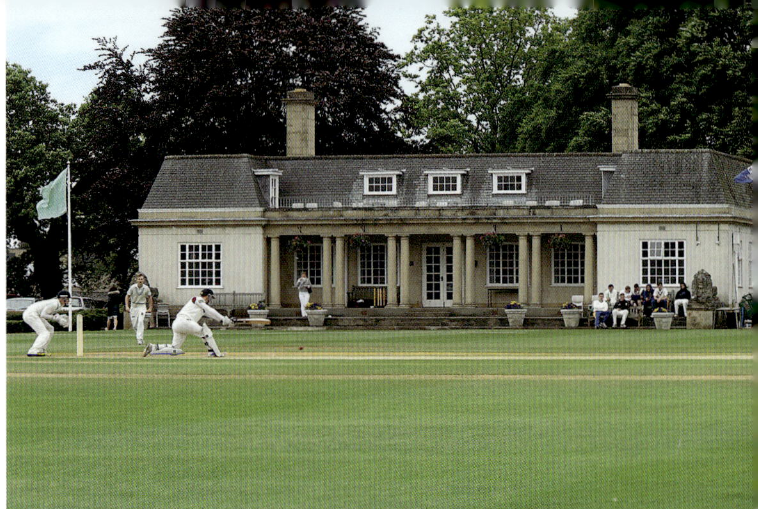

move of their twentieth-century replacements to the School Chapel plinths has been one of the greatest achievements of the restoration that is the subject of the fourth chapter in Stowe's story.

A Future Inspired by the Past

Just like the House in its heyday as the seat of a great political dynasty, development of the site as a centre of learning has rarely stood still since the School's foundation. An art school in the Brutalist style of the 1930s, a cricket pavilion in the very best traditions of Edwardian architecture, technology and science blocks that reflect the style of the 1960s, further boarding accommodation built in the 1970s and yet more in the early part of the twenty-first century, and the 2014 award-winning Music School that is cleverly situated to respond to the lines and setting of the historic gardens, are developments by the School in response to evolving business demands and standards. Work continues, not only to expand and progress, but also to harmonise and mitigate the impact of less attractive buildings on a site of such beauty and significance.

But the greatest step of all in this meandering journey was the way in which the Governors of the School and the National Trust facilitated the rescue and restoration of not just the House but also the Landscape Gardens. Having held back the ravages of time on the infrastructure and façades of the House and watched the Landscape Gardens become steadily eroded by the remorseless advance of nature, the Governors had to act. Clear that neither Gardens nor House could be rescued within the modest revenues of a Public School, and with the help of an anonymous benefactor about whom more later, Stowe and the National Trust entered into an agreement in 1989 that saw the National Trust take on the Landscape Gardens subject to the School's right to use the land granted to the National Trust for centuries to come. The achievements of the National Trust over the last 25 years are testament to the wisdom and far-sightedness of this decision. Some 10 years later, in 1999, with parts of the House beginning to crumble and fall, the Governors with the National Trust conjured up another imaginative solution and created the Stowe House Preservation Trust (SHPT), a body independent of the School that was charged with the stewardship of the House and its restoration. Helped by enormous generosity, and the anonymous benefactor once again, the SHPT was able to access a variety of funding, including the World Monuments Fund (WMF) and The Heritage Lottery Fund. In just 10 years this has enabled the SHPT to see the restoration of the main fabric of the House.

Stowe Avenue is symbolic of the way in which the Estate has been saved and continues to prosper under the National

OPPOSITE
The 1930s Art School (left), restored by the School in 2010, and the Edwardian cricket pavilion (right).

RIGHT
The Award-winning 2014 Music School (by architect Nick Cox), shaped to respond to the historic lines of the Landscape Gardens.

BELOW RIGHT
Furnished for twenty-first century educational needs, the Library retains its eighteenth-century mahogany bookcases.

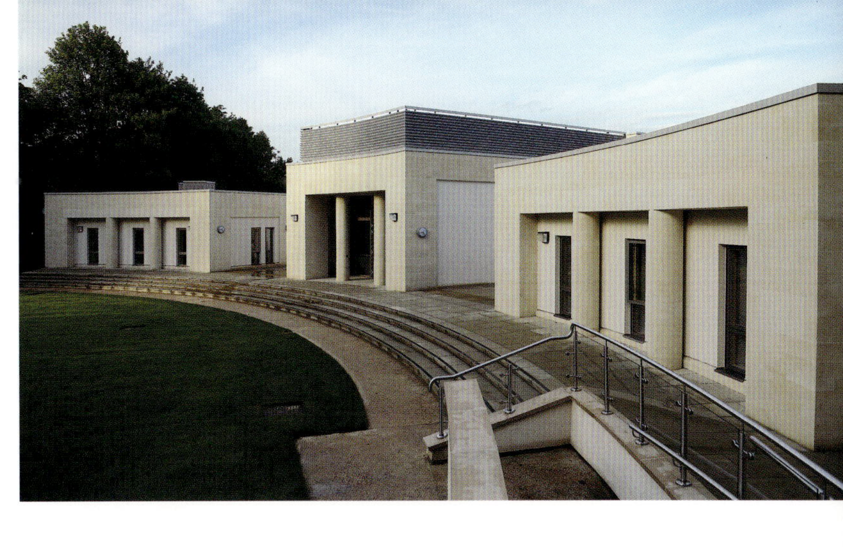

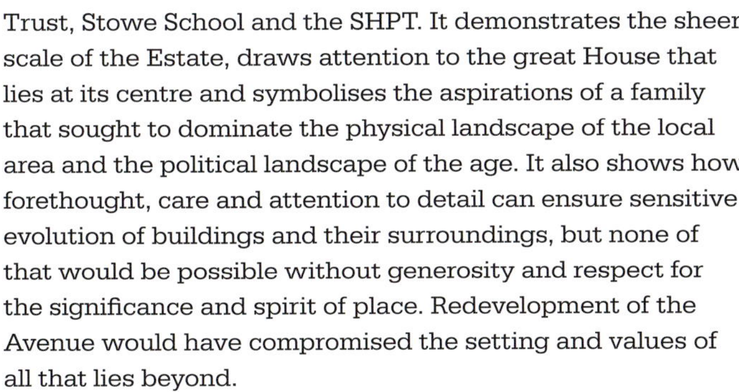

Trust, Stowe School and the SHPT. It demonstrates the sheer scale of the Estate, draws attention to the great House that lies at its centre and symbolises the aspirations of a family that sought to dominate the physical landscape of the local area and the political landscape of the age. It also shows how forethought, care and attention to detail can ensure sensitive evolution of buildings and their surroundings, but none of that would be possible without generosity and respect for the significance and spirit of place. Redevelopment of the Avenue would have compromised the setting and values of all that lies beyond.

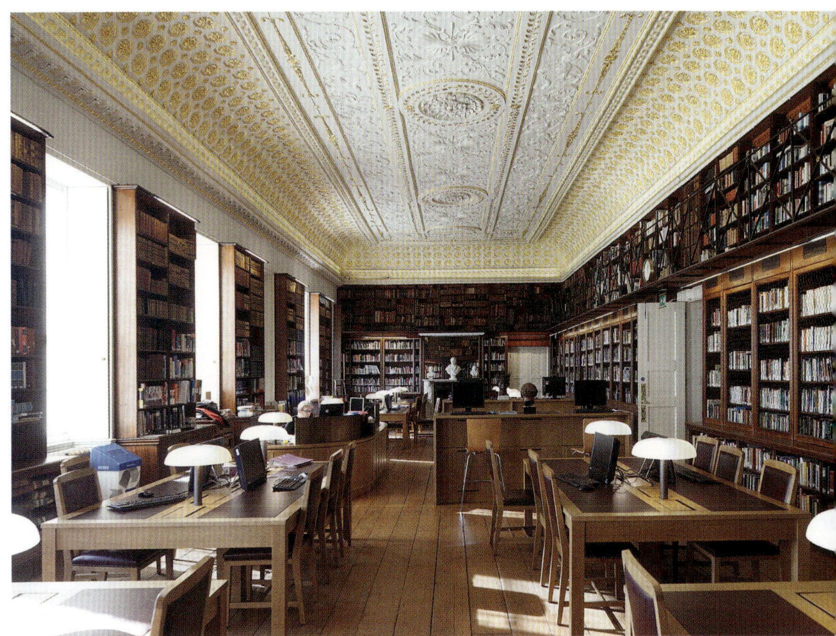

NOTES

6 Clough Williams-Ellis, *Architect Errant* (London, 1971, reprinted 1980), pp. 139–40.

7 Ibid.

8 Noel Annan, *Roxburgh of Stowe: The Life of J.F. Roxburgh and His Influence in the Public Schools* (London, 1965), p. 58.

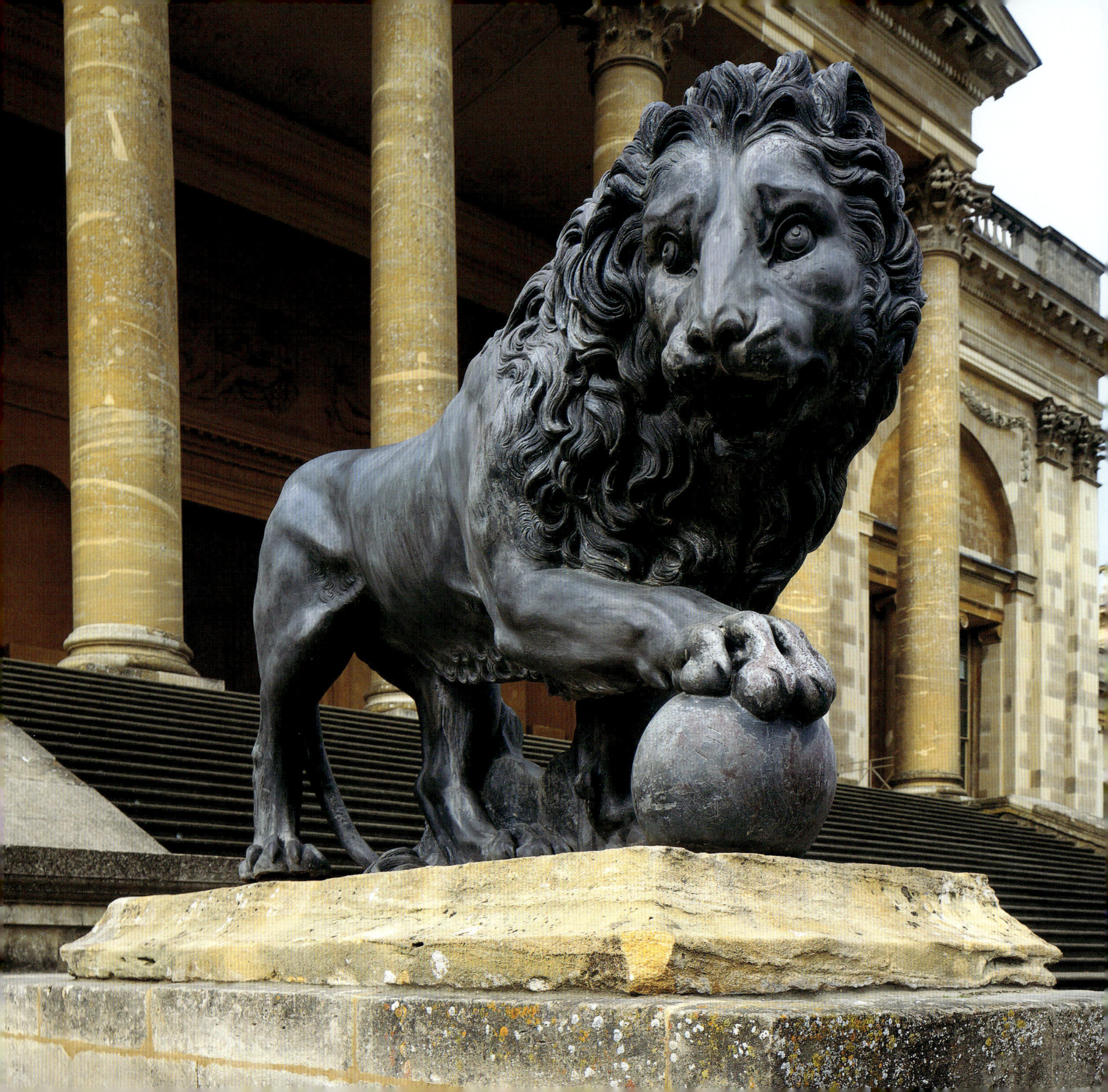

4 RESTORATION

If Stowe's creation was rooted in the essence and principles of the eighteenth century, its restoration, which began in 2000, has been characterised by no less a spirit of generosity and innovation. As befits the largest private Neo-Classical building in Europe, the programme has been of monumental proportions, costing in excess of £40m, and has seen the involvement of expert craftsmen and women with skills worthy of the very best of their forebears. The aim has been to return the House to its appearance in its heyday at the end of the eighteenth century.

Restoration was planned in six phases and the saving of Stowe was supported by a number of publicly funded bodies and charitable trusts. However, equally important has been the largesse of individuals, most notably the anonymous benefactor who made significant donations subject to 'matched funding' being raised. 'Watch listing' by the WMF in 2002 drew attention to the plight of Stowe House. The WMF helped by raising £5m, thus securing a total of £10m when matched by the anonymous donor.

OPPOSITE
Returned to Stowe in 2013, one of the Medici lions.

RIGHT
High above the South Front, the heraldic figures have been restored to their former glory.

In July 2000 work started on the North Front, and was completed on time and to budget in September 2002, without any disruption to the School and, happily, with no health and safety issues arising from the combination of inquisitive youngsters and a tempting building site. The WMF 'watch listing' proved to be instrumental in securing funding for a second phase of the restoration in 2002. Having visited Stowe *incognito*, Robert Wilson, an American philanthropist and long-time supporter of the WMF, offered to contribute towards restoration of the great Marble Saloon at the centre of the enfilade of State Rooms. The first task was to remove tanks containing 60,000 litres of water from directly above the Marble Saloon. The consequences for

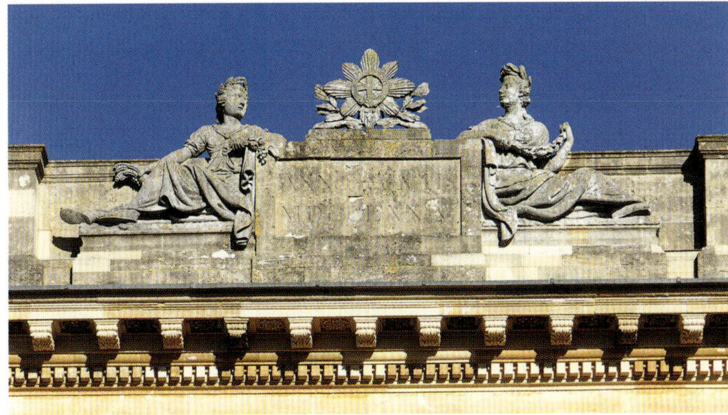

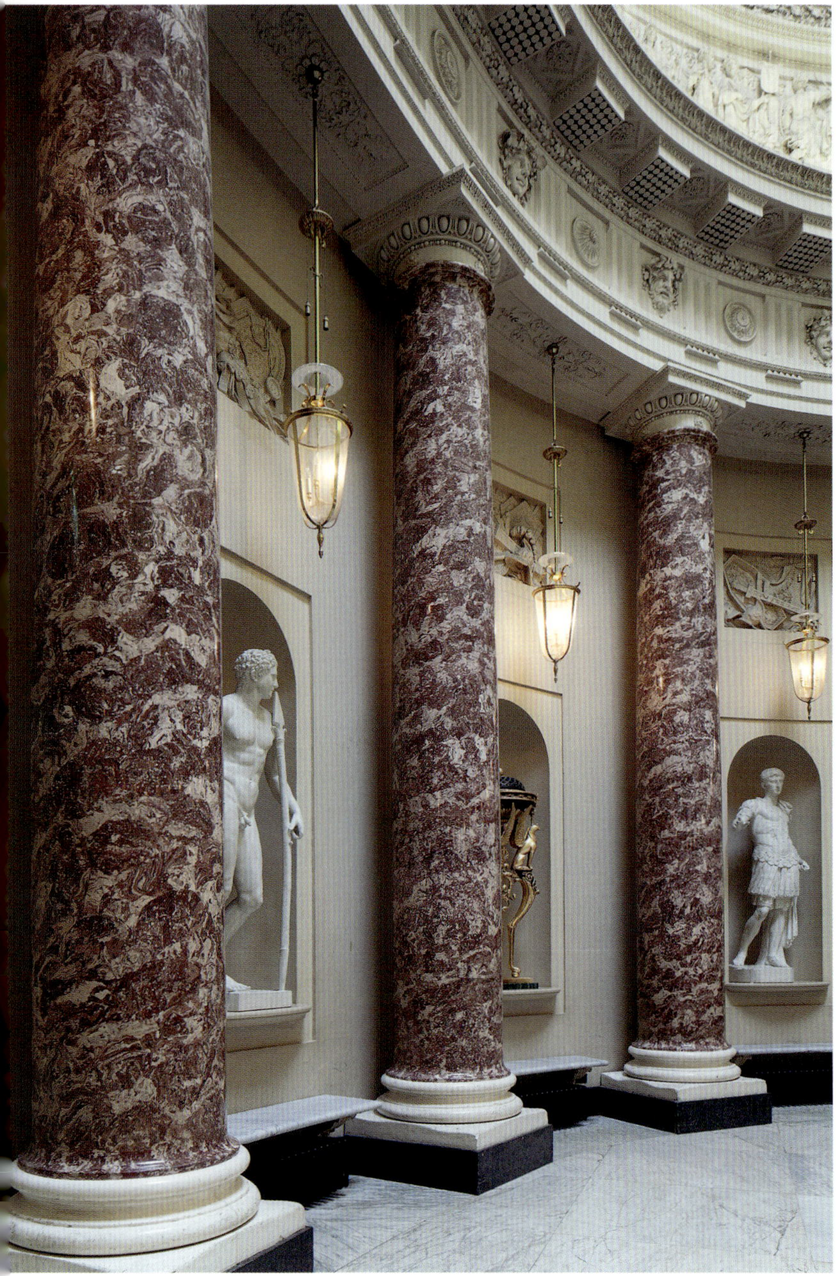

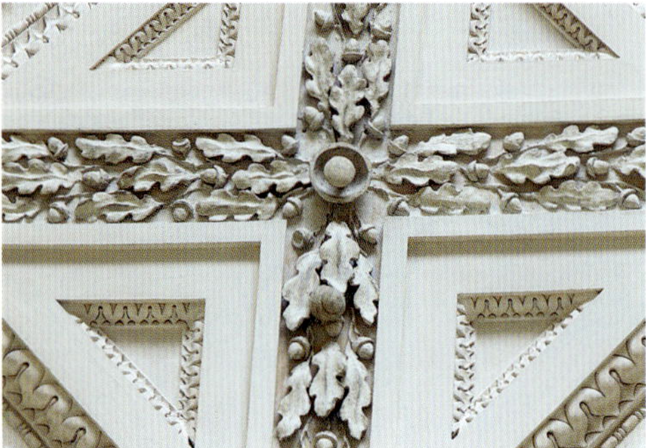

LEFT
Scagliola was re-applied to the Marble Saloon's columns during restoration.

ABOVE
A tennis ball was found high up during restoration of the Marble Saloon and was included as part of the finished work.

the plaster ceiling below of those tanks failing do not bear contemplation. The rebuilding of the dome over the Saloon then began. A scaffolded roof was erected over the whole central area, which, at 55 metres by 45 metres, was the largest of its type ever constructed. Life went on underneath this structure with occupants protected by a 'crash deck' and an insulated ceiling providing some material comforts. This phase was completed in 2005 and attention turned to the restoration of the entire South Front.

September 2011 marked another milestone when completion of work to the South Front meant that, for the first time in 12 years, the House stood on its own without scaffolding. In a two-year project, the contractor replaced 60 cubic metres of stone on the east side and 80 cubic metres on the west side of the House, re-roofed the Library and replaced all the cracked and damaged render. Resplendent in the late summer sunshine, the restored stonework and newly applied render once more justify the epithet 'grandest temple in the landscape' and stand witness to the exceptional generosity of the benefactors and talent of the craftspeople involved. This part of the restoration cost £6m and again an

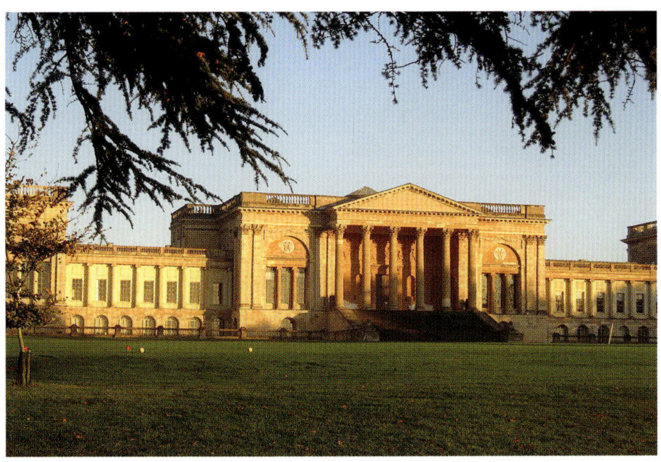

South Front in the late summer sunshine.

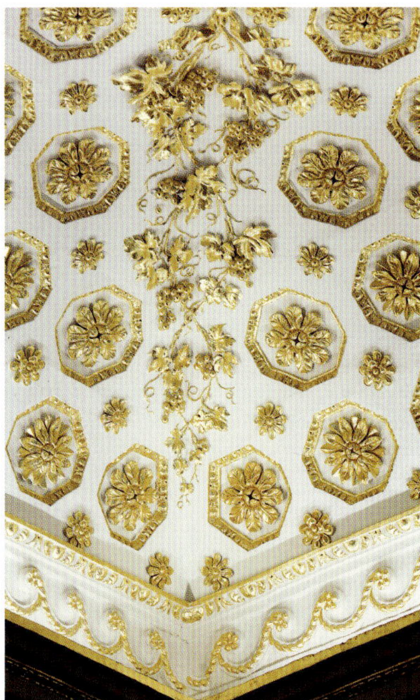

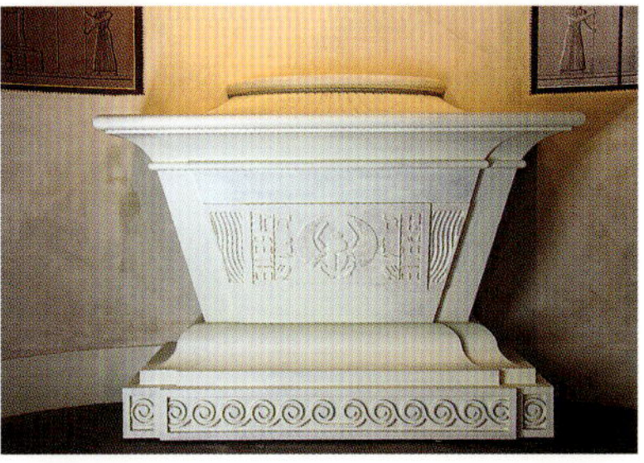

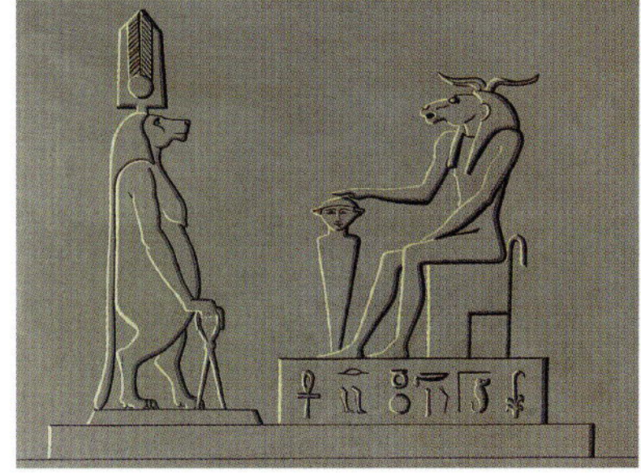

RIGHT
Detail of gilding on the Library ceiling.

BELOW
The replica sarcophagus with its hieroglyphics in the Egyptian Hall. While in 1803 hieroglyphics were not understood, Stowe opted to use the Temple-Grenville motto 'How beautiful are thy temples'.

BOTTOM
Representations of the images that would once have filled the niches in the walls of the Egyptian Hall add to the authenticity of its appearance.

imaginative solution from the partners at Stowe came to the rescue. Through a multi-party arrangement the funding was gained to finance this restoration, while at the same time the School agreed to build a new golf course to the east of the Estate enabling the National Trust to restore the Western Garden.

The Library had to be vacated by the School to allow the construction of a new roof to replace a twentieth-century flat roof and restoration of its delicate ceiling. As conservators set to work on the plaster, they discovered traces of gilding beneath the top seven layers of paint. Microscopic analysis of 286 samples through successive paint layers revealed the presence of gold leaf in the sixth of 13 paint schemes. A panel of experts decided that the borders and rosettes should be regilded, leaving the figures on the ceiling in a natural colour. It was estimated that 30,000 leaves of 23.5 carat gold would be required; interestingly, archival research of the House accounts found that in the 1790s 28,500 leaves had been purchased.

The Egyptian Hall had long been a neglected space despite being significant as one of the first Egyptian-inspired

The *Dance of the Hours*, with a detail of the restored horses opposite.

interiors in an English country house. Painstaking analysis of the wall surfaces revealed traces of sand in the original paintwork, added to give a depth of realism to the architect's work of re-creating the appearance of an Egyptian temple for the House's winter entrance. With a replica sarcophagus, sphinxes to guard the staircase up to the North Hall and modern representations of the paintings that graced the temple's wall niches and the central portion of the ceiling, the Hall assumed an authentic appearance once more.

In 2012 work started on the magnificent State Music Room, with the aim of achieving a balanced renovation that lifted the original paintwork while toning down the impact of a partial restoration from the 1970s. In the process, more unseen gilding and decorative details were discovered and reinstated. The circular painting at the centre of the ceiling, a copy of the *Dance of the Hours* painted by Vincenzo Valdrè for the Marquess of Buckingham in 1788, presented a particular challenge. Valdrè's original had been sold in 1922 and a copy made in the 1970s. Sold again in the 1970s, the original's location was unknown. An unexpected telephone call in October 2012 revealed that the painting was to come up at auction and the SHPT bought it. After inspection, it was sent to specialist conservators. The story, though, carries a twist. Evidence showed that the room had been illuminated in the eighteenth century by a central chandelier that, it was assumed, had been installed at the same time as the painting. Early investigation cast doubt on this until detailed examination of the artist's work confirmed that a fixing for a light fitting had existed and that the painting had been completed by the original artist with a fitting in situ. Such details illustrate the extent of research needed to guarantee the authenticity of restoration work.

Another chance telephone call in August 2011 presented a surprising opportunity. Blackpool Corporation contacted the WMF to suggest the possibility of returning to Stowe the lions that had once guarded the South Front entrance. The lions had found their way to Blackpool after a philanthropist purchased them in 1922 and gave them to the town for

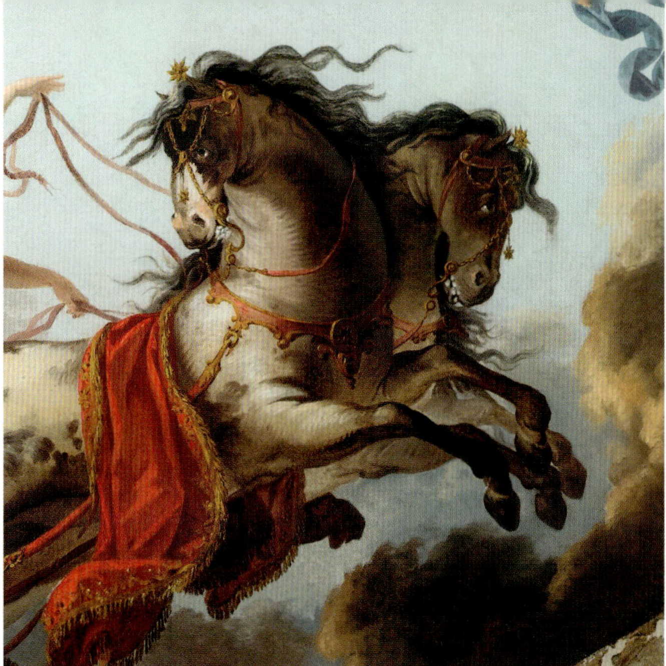

BELOW
Gently does it: a lion takes his rightful place at the South Front entrance.

BOTTOM
The inscription showing that this lion is a copy of one carved by the Italian Flaminio Vacca.

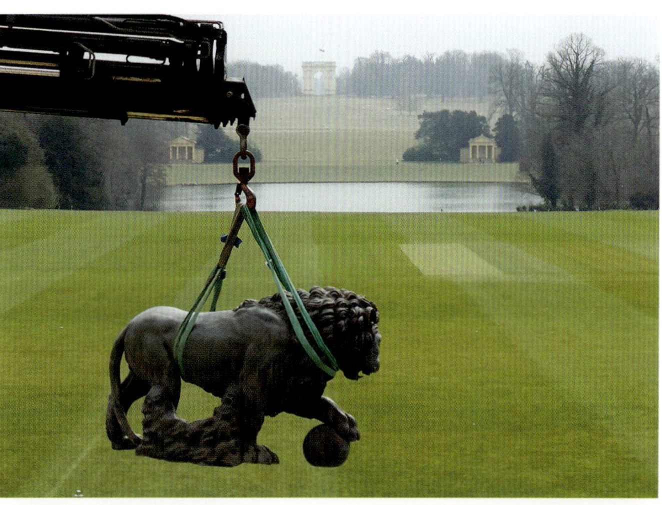

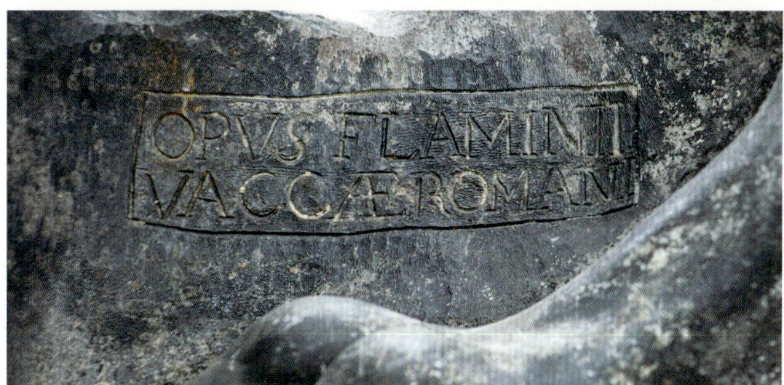

display in Stanley Park. Concerned that they were vulnerable to metal theft, the Corporation proposed lending the lions to Stowe in return for exact copies. An agreement was drawn up and a spell of 'therapy' in a conservation workshop restored the spring to the lions' step so that, on a crisp bright day in April 2013, they set out on the last stage of the journey home to take their rightful place, guarding the entrance that has welcomed visitors since the eighteenth century.

The lions themselves are copies of marble statues that now stand outside the Loggia dei Lanzi in Florence having been commissioned for the Villa Medici in Rome. Although a matched pair, they come from different parentage. The lion to the west of the steps is copied from an antique lion apparently cut from a relief sculpture by Sciarono in the sixteenth century, while the second was sculpted by Flaminio Vacca in 1594. An inscription recording Vacca's work has been reproduced in the lead and can be seen today on the outside face of the base of the eastern lion.

John Bickerdike's 'Jazz Age' lions, referred to by Clough Williams-Ellis as 'Utility Lions', were relocated from the South Front to the plinths of the School Chapel, where they blend well with the contemporary style of the interior and complement the iconography of the exterior.

The Blue Room, which since its creation in the 1740s has served as a billiard room, breakfast room, print room, drawing room and common room for younger boys, takes its name from the 1860s when blue silk damask was hung

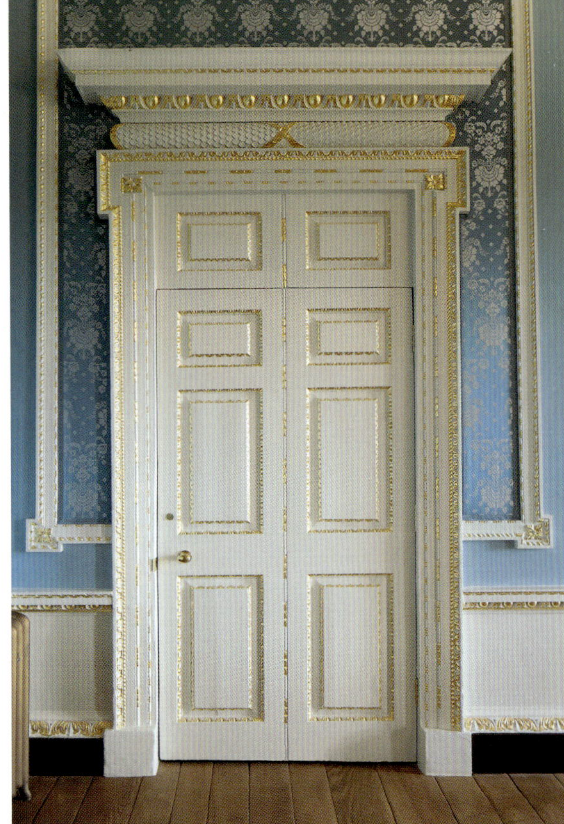

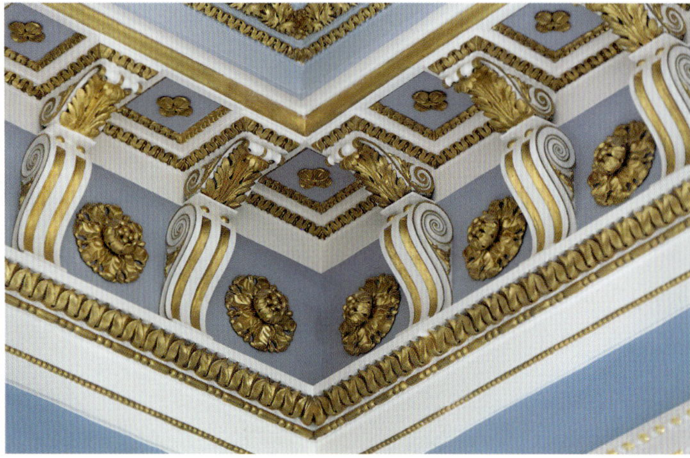

LEFT
Blue silk damask and gold leaf: opulence restored to the Blue Room.

ABOVE
Replastered, repainted and re-gilded, the details of the Blue Room once more reflect its Victorian splendour.

OPPOSITE
William Kent's depiction of Lord Cobham and King William III on the North Hall ceiling restored in 2015.

on the walls between gilded frames. Photographic evidence showed the room as it had appeared then and, although out of line with restoration of the rest of the House to the late eighteenth century, this scheme was selected as the most appropriate for showing the final flourish of the family trying to regain some of the status and influence it had enjoyed in the heyday of the House. Archival research identified the closest match for the damask, which was then woven at one of the few remaining silk manufacturers in this country, possibly the source of the original fabric. Detailed investigation tempered with fine architectural judgement defined the extent of the wall panels and, with the ceiling cleaned, the walls replastered and painted in the correct colours, the room has taken its place alongside grandeurs from an earlier age.

Work continues at Stowe with the restoration of the grand entrance in the North Hall but, in closing this chapter, it is fitting to reflect on the skills of the stonemasons, plasterers, joiners and others who represent the latest generation in a long tradition of craftsmen and women determined to deliver work that is worthy of one of the greatest houses in the country and assure its resurrection for the education and delight of future generations. At the height of the restoration, 29 stonemasons worked on the exteriors of Stowe, while painting conservators, on and off site, carpenters, joiners and metal workers, bricklayers, gilders and plasterers, plumbers and electricians all brought traditional skills of the highest quality. Without them and the benefactors, architects, surveyors, safety specialists, engineers and project managers, none of this restoration would have been possible.

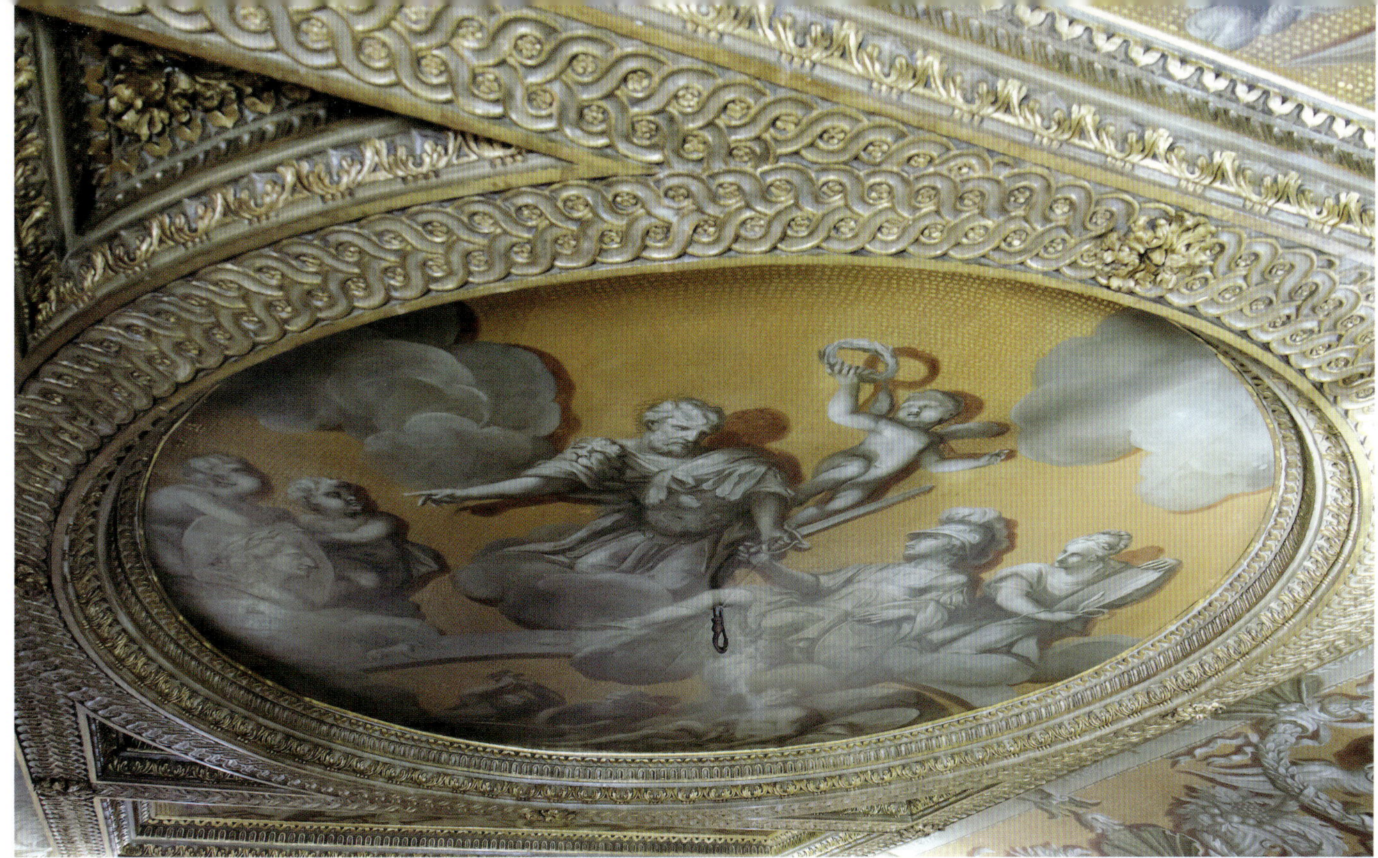

FURTHER READING

Stowe House
Michael Bevington, *Stowe House* (London, 2002).

Contemporary Accounts of Stowe
George Clarke (ed.), *Descriptions of Lord Cobham's Gardens at Stowe 1700–1750* (Buckinghamshire Record Society, 1990).

Photographic Record
Anthony Meredith, *Stowe Through Time* (Stroud, 2009).

Landscape Gardens
John Martin Robinson, *Temples of Delight: Stowe Landscape Gardens* (London, 1990).

National Trust, *Stowe Landscape Gardens: A Comprehensive Guide* (Swindon, 1999, revised 2005).

National Trust, *Stowe* (Swindon, 2011) (abridged garden tours).

The Temple-Grenvilles
John Beckett, *The Rise and Fall of the Grenvilles, Dukes of Buckingham and Chandos 1770 to 1921* (Manchester, 1994).

Jonathan Roberts and Gerard Morgan-Grenville, *No Ordinary Tourist: The Travels of an Errant Duke* (Bridport, 2006).

Ophelia Field, *The Kit-Cat Club: Friends Who Imagined a Nation* (London, 2008).

Michale Bevington (with George Clarke, Tim Knox and Jonathan Marsden) (ed. Oliver Garnett), *Stowe: The People and the Place* (London, 2011).

On Stowe School and Clough Williams-Ellis
Noel Annan, *Roxburgh of Stowe: The Life of J.F. Roxburgh and His Influence in the Public Schools* (London, 1965).

Clough Williams-Ellis, *Architect Errant* (London, 1971).

Brian Rees, *Stowe: The History of a Public School 1923–1988* (London, 2008).

TOUR OF STOWE HOUSE

The Visitor Entrance to Stowe House is today on the South Front, beneath the Temple Room, opening directly into a Welcome Centre where once was the Servants' Hall. A doorway created in 2015 leads into the cellar, allowing visitors a unique view upwards that reveals the secrets of construction of the Marble Saloon above. The cellar contains audio-visual displays and exhibitions as a prelude to the visit to the State Rooms. Leaving the cellar, visitors cross the service corridor now known as Plug Street and enter the Egyptian Hall. Installed in 1803 below the North Hall, it was designed by the Marquess of Buckingham to look like the Egyptian Temple of Dendra, featuring a painted reproduction of the Temple's zodiac frieze and interpretations of the Egyptian style decoration selected by the Marquess. The Egyptian Hall served as the winter entrance to the House. The State Rooms are on the upper floor, known as the Piano Nobile, and reached via the North Hall from the stone stairs guarded by two sphinxes.

The North Hall's magnificent painted ceiling shows Viscount Cobham dressed as a Roman Emperor receiving a sword from King William III depicted as Mars, the god of war. Painted on a gold mosaic background using grisaille, a technique that represents objects in relief by the use of grey shadowing, the ceiling is the work of William Kent from 1734. Military trophies adorn the coving.

From the North Hall, the East Corridor passes beneath the Grand Staircase with its ceiling by Francesco Sleter depicting *Fame and Victory* and into the Ante-Library. The State Rooms are reached through the Blue Room, restored as it would have appeared in the 1860s. Beyond it lie a former State Bedchamber (now the Green Drawing Room) and Dressing Room (now the Victoria Room), both used by Queen Victoria. These now serve as dormitories and are open to visitors when not in use by the School.

The Library retains its original mahogany bookcases with their distinctive wire fronts, restored in 2010. The gilded ceiling is from about 1793, although parts date from the room's original layout as a Ballroom in the 1740s.

The State Music Room features delicate Pompeian-style wall paintings by Vincenzo Valdrè, with playful scenes of *amoretti* (chubby winged male babies), young girls and garlands among which flowers, butterflies and birds abound. The central painting, *Dance of the Hours*, was re-acquired in 2012 and carefully restored.

The Marble Saloon is the heart of the house about which the symmetrical layout is articulated. Inspired by the Pantheon in Rome, at 17 metres high it is an impressive structure. The coffers (sunken square ornamental panels) are bound together by oak leaves representing victory, while the frieze portrays a Roman procession, continuing the martial theme from George I's equestrian statue on the North Front, through the North Hall and out to the triumphal Corinthian Arch at the southern end of the Landscape Gardens. It contains 280 human figures, 14 animals and two trophies (Michael Bevington, *Stowe House* [London, 2002], p. 36). The room takes its name from the floor of Carrara marble.

The Temple Room, whose dimensions exactly mirror those of the State Music Room to the east, has a Neo-Classical ceiling attributed to Valdrè. Originally this was the State Drawing Room, much admired by Queen Victoria, and contained paintings by Peter Paul Rubens, Joshua Reynolds and Nicolas Poussin. The State Dining Room (formerly the State Gallery) has a ceiling in grisaille, with central paintings by Robert Jones replacing earlier work by Francesco Sleter, whose work on the cove remains. Beyond the State Dining Room lie the former State Dressing Room and, at the far western end of the house, the former State Bedchamber (now the Garter Room), where the insignia of the Order of the Garter in relief on the ceiling marks the granting of the Garter to Earl Temple in February 1760.